Assessments and Lesson Plans

for

Graves, Juel, and Graves

Teaching Reading in the 21ˢᵗ Century

Third Edition

prepared by

Kathleen M. Wilson
University of Nebraska, Lincoln

Robert C. Calfee
University of California, Riverside

Michael F. Graves
University of Minnesota

Guy Trainin
University of Nebraska, Lincoln

PEARSON

Boston   New York   San Francisco
Mexico City   Montreal   Toronto   London   Madrid   Munich   Paris
Hong Kong   Singapore   Tokyo   Cape Town   Sydney

ISBN 0-205-40739-0

Printed in the United States of America

10 9 8 7 6 5 4 3 2 1   08 07 06 05 04 03

The SRE lesson plans for "And the Dish Ran Away with the Spoon," *Because of Winn-Dixie*, and "Black Powder," pp. 80-142, are taken from the OnLine Reading Resources web site onlinereadingresources.com © 2003 by Seward Incorporated and are reprinted with the permission of Seward Incorporated.

Table of Contents

Part One: Assessments

Part Two: Lesson Plans

Introduction to the Assessments

Tile Test

The <u>Tile Test</u> is an assessment of emergent and early reading skills. It is administered individually and is used with students in the primary grades. The assessment begins with the student being asked to identify a subset of the letters of the alphabet and their letter-sound relationships using letter tiles that are commonly found in primary grade classrooms. Next, the teacher builds real and synthetic words to assess the student's skill at decoding. Meta-language and articulation questions are used to understand the student's strategies for decoding unknown words. The student is then asked to build real and synthetic words to measure his spelling skills. Meta-language and articulation questions similar to those in the decoding section are asked to determine the student's strategies for spelling. Word recognition of sight words is assessed with a set of word tiles. The student reads the words as the tiles are placed in front of him. Then, the teacher builds short sentences with the word tiles and has the student to read the sentences. Finally, the student builds sentences that the teacher dictates to him.

Graduated Running Record

The <u>Graduated Running Record</u> is a tool that teachers use to assess students' oral reading accuracy, fluency, and comprehension. This assessment is administered on an individual basis. Two formats are offered – one at a pre-primer/primer level and the other that ranges from a mid 1st grade to a 6th grade reading level. Both formats include a retelling of the story to check for comprehension. The advantage that the <u>Graduated Running Record</u> has over other running records is that each sentence in the paragraph becomes progressively more difficult, making the assessment a quick and efficient way to determine students' skill at reading.

Interactive Reading Assessment System – Revised (IRAS –R)

The <u>IRAS – R</u> is an informal reading inventory that is appropriate for use with students from mid-year 1st grade to junior high school. It is comprised of a series of subtests that can be used to assess one or more reading skills. The array of skills that can be measured include alphabet recognition, letter-sound relationships, real word recognition, vocabulary level, synthetic word decoding and spelling, sentence reading, oral and silent comprehension, and listening comprehension. Both narrative and expository passages are included to determine whether the student demonstrates differences in comprehension between stories and informational text.

Read-Write Cycle Assessments

The <u>Read-Write Cycle Assessments</u> give teachers a template with which they can develop writing assessments that determine the best writing a student can do on a given topic. These assessments have been used successfully with mainstream and struggling readers and writers from second grade through high school. Unlike the more common on-demand writing assessments with formats that differ from typical classroom instruction, <u>Read-Write Cycle Assessments</u> are embedded within two regular class periods. Students participate in pre-writing activities that include reading a short passage and use cooperative/collaborative instructional strategies to scaffold each student's prior knowledge about the topic. Whole class, small group, and individual formats are used as the student gets ready to write. Following the pre-writing activities, students are given two related prompts from which to choose to focus their writing.

An analytic rubric is included for scoring the final essays. The rubric is developmentally-based. It includes separate ratings for length, coherence, vocabulary, and grammar/mechanics/ spelling. This scoring system clearly highlights students' writing strengths and weaknesses, helping the teacher to make future instructional choices that fit the needs of her class.

Text Maps

Two types of <u>Text Maps</u> – "Story Notes" and "Report Notes" - are offered as tools for teachers to observe students' thinking as they analyze features of a variety of passages. Additionally, the <u>Text Maps</u> can be used by students to plan for writing stories, reports, research papers, and summaries. "Story Notes" are designed for use with narrative text, while "Report Notes" examines the features of exposition.

Tile Test

Grade Level: Kindergarten – 2nd Grade

The Tile Test is designed to quickly assess students' understanding of letters, sounds, words, and sentences. Meta-linguistic questions encourage students to talk about the strategies they use when decoding and spelling words.

General Procedures

1. Start with a collection of letter tiles, not just one card.
2. Allow sufficient time for each response.
3. Provide general positive feedback to encourage students, do not correct mistakes.
4. Write the students' responses to each item:
   - a. Correct response is marked + or Π,
   - b. Incorrect responses will be recorded in full,
   - c. No response will be recorded as dk (Doesn't Know),
   - d. Self Correction is marked SC and counted as correct.
   - e. Segmented words read without blending sounds will be marked with slashes between sounds e.g. /t/a/p/.
5. Administer all components.
5. Stop Rule, if a student is unable to respond to any word of the first 4 items use teacher judgment to discontinue this segment and move to the next. If a student is unsuccessful in reading the word tiles at all do not proceed to sentence reading.

Letters and Sounds

Begin with a collection of letter tiles [**m, a, p, i, f, s, t, d, n**].
1. Have students point to the letter you name.
2. Ask students to tell you the <u>name</u> and <u>sound</u> of each letter.

Words

Add the following letters to the collection of letter tiles [h, e, w, c, k, v, u, l, s, o, d, d, b, r, p, g].
1. Manipulate individual letters to build the given words. The teacher builds, and the student reads. Follow-up with the Articulation and Metalinguistic (ML) questions below.
2. Ask the student to use the letter tiles to build the words you read. (Articulation and ML) Record student responses. Observe and record strategy use (i.e., orally articulating sounds) and behaviors.
3. Use the word tiles provided on a separate sheet to assess word reading, Leave word tiles on the table for use in the next section.

<u>**Metalinguistic (ML) and Articulation Questions**</u>: Following the reading of 'pat' and 'sat' and the building of 'tan' and 'tad,' ask how the student knew to make the change(s) he or she made. After the successful reading or building of their most difficult word, ask the student what his or her mouth did to say the first sound of the word. Then ask how he or she knew to read / build the word that way? Record student responses. Provide and document probing questions as necessary. (Examples: What were you looking at? I noticed your mouth moving, how did that help you?) Score the ML questions using the Tile Test Meta-language Rubric.

Sentences

Use the collection of words to create sentences. Record student responses.
1. Using the word cards, build each sentence and have the student read.
2. Ask the student to use the word cards to build sentences you read. Then ask the student to read the sentence they built. Record student responses.
3. Hand the student the sentence on the separate sheet and have the student read it. Record student responses.

Tile Test Meta-Language Rubric

0	No Response; "I don't know"
1	"I know it." "My mom taught me." "I'm smart."
2	Recognition of letters; "I looked at the letters."
3	Recognition of sounds; "I sound it out." " I listen to the sounds."
4	Partial linking sounds to letters; "It starts with a P /p/, then /l/ " Or Partial analogy "Pat is like cat"
5	Explains spelling of <u>each</u> sound. Or full analogy "Pat is like cat, but it starts with a /p/."
6	Explains how sounds are articulated. "It starts with /p/ my lips are together and the air pops out, my tongue is resting in the middle of my mouth…".

Tile Test: Recording Sheet

Student _____Date _____School_____Teacher_____

Letter Identification: Lay out letter tiles [**m, a, p, i, f, s, t, d, n**].
"Here are some letters. I'll say the name of a letter and ask you to point to the letter. Point to the card that has the letter m." (*Record, continue procedure*)
"Now, I'll point to a card and you'll tell me two things about the letter. First, the <u>name</u> of the letter, and second, the <u>sound</u> that it makes." (*Record*)

	Identification	Name	Sound			Identification	Name	Sound
m					s			
a					t			
p					d			
i					n			

Words:
Add these letter tiles to the tiles above: [**b, c, d, d, e, h, k, l, o, r, r, s, u, v, w**].
"Now let's put some letters together to make words. Some of the words are real words and some are pretend words. I'll go first and make a word, and then I'll ask you to read it for me." (*Manipulate only necessary letters, stop after sat and ask the first ML & articulation questions.*)

↓**pat** _____	**vute** _____
***sat** _____	**flass** _____
sam _____	**lodded** _____
hin _____	**wembick** _____

*ML: "I noticed that you said 'sat' (*or repeat what the student said if different*). How did you know to change it that way from 'pat' (*or repeat what the student said*)?"_____
_____
_____

Articulation: "Tell me what your mouth did to say the first sound in_____ ." (*Repeat the most difficult word they read correctly.*) Record verbal responses and behaviors.

_____
_____

(Use the most difficult word decoded correctly)
ML: "How did you know to say _____ that way?_____
_____
_____

_____
"Now, I'll say a word, and you make it for me." (*As you dictate, clearly articulate by "stretching" each sound. Example: tan = /t/ /_/ /n/, stop after tad and ask the first ML and articulation questions.*)

↓**tan** _____	**plat** _____
***tad** _____	**mape** _____
tap _____	**pridder** _____
leb _____	**radmin** _____

*ML: "How did you know to change [the 'n' to a 'd']? (*Use the letter changes the student has made.*)_____
_____

Articulation: "Tell me what my mouth did to help you spell _____ ." (*Repeat the most difficult word they spelled correctly.*) Record verbal responses and behaviors.

_____

_____

(Use the most difficult word spelled correctly)
ML: "How did you know to spell _____ that way?_____

_____

Words:
Lay out the collection of word cards [**I, me, the, a, is, at, look, dog, cat, big, map, can, sat, fat, sit, on, run**].
"I'll show you some words, and you read each one." (*Record, and if incorrect, say the right word,*)

I _____   me _____   the_____   a_____

is _____   at _____   look _____   dog _____

cat _____   big _____   map _____   can _____

sat _____   fat _____   sit _____   on _____

run _____

Sentences:
"I'll make a sentence with some words, and you read the sentence for me."
I can run.   _____

Look at me.   _____

I sat on the cat.   _____

The map is big.   _____

Sit the dog on the fat cat. _____

"Now I'll say a sentence, and you can make it for me." [Have the student read the sentence after building it.] (*Record sentence made and the student's read of it.*)

I can sit.   _____

The dog is fat.   _____

Look at the map.   _____

A dog can look at me.   _____

The big cat sat on the dog. _____

"Now I want you to read one sentence for me." (*Give the student the sheet with the sentence printed on it. Record the student's reading.*)

General Observations: _____

_____

Tile Test Words

Copy this page cut (laminate) for use in word and sentence reading segments.

| I | . | at | me | . |

| look | the | dog | a | . |

| cat | is | big | . |

| map | on | can | . |

| run | sat | Look | . |

| fat | Sit | sit | The |

Graduated Running Record

The Graduated Running Record is an assessment that allows a teacher to systematically observe what a child does as he or she reads connected text aloud. It brings to the forefront the student's use of the semantic, syntactic, and graphophonemic cuing system, enabling the teacher to quickly determine areas of strength and weakness.

The Graduated Running Record is formatted in a manner that minimizes the time commitment needed to individually assess an elementary class. Each version offers one paragraph on an interesting Social Studies, Science, or narrative topic. The Early Reading Format assesses young students' reading at the pre-primer/primer level. In the two Elementary Level Formats each of the seven sentences in the passage increases in difficulty from the previous sentence. Starting the passage at a mid-first grade level, the sentences advance in difficulty by grade, with the final sentence reflecting a sixth grade reading level. The average time needed to administer varies with the reading level of the child, but should not exceed 90 seconds. Since comprehension is jeopardized when fluency is poor, the 90 second stop limit is used as one criterion for ending the reading. A second stop limit is based on the number of grade level words missed in a sentence.

Teachers can evaluate each student's employment of the semantic, syntactic and graphophonemic cuing systems, aiding them to individualize instruction and promote optimal growth in reading. This knowledge is gained by evaluating the total amount of text read in the allotted time for fluency and the types of substitutions, omissions, and self corrections the child makes while reading the passage aloud to the teacher. Comprehension for each Format is assessed by having the student retell the story.

GRADUATED RUNNING RECORD ADMINISTRATION GUIDE

The Graduated Running Record assesses accuracy, fluency, prosody, and comprehension from pre-primer and primer levels in the Early Reading Format, and the middle Grade One level to the Grade Six level in the Elementary Level Formats. In the Elementary Level Formats the first sentence is a measure of the middle Grade One level, while the second sentence assesses the reading level for the end of Grade One. Each of the following sentences advances a grade, with the third sentence at Grade Two and the last sentence assessing Grade Six. The Early Reading Format assess.

Directions:

Read the title of the passage to the student and direct him or her to read the passage aloud to you. Tell the student:

"I would like you to read this story aloud to me. As you read I will be making marks on my page to remember what you say. It is important that you know that the words in the story will be getting harder with each sentence. I may ask you to stop reading before you have finished the story. If you have not finished reading the story, I will read the rest of the story to you. After you finish reading, I will ask you to tell me what you remember from the story."

Use the recording sheet to note everything the child says. Specific notations are used in the following manner:

Assessing Fluency

Accurate reading: Every correct response is denoted with a Y.
Repetition: (not to be counted as an error) Underline the repeated word, phrase, or sentence.
Substitutions: Use a ∧ to indicate a substituted word. Write the substituted word above the caret. Substitutions are counted as errors.
Self-corrections: (not to be counted as an error) Write the incorrect pronunciation of the word. Then write SC next to the word.

Omissions: Draw a line through an omitted word. Omissions are counted as errors. (If the student is trying to decode the word, let them continue. If they have given up on the word, tell the child the word.)

1. Stop the assessment when the child has four or more errors (underlined words only) in a
2. Using only <u>UNDERLINED</u> words on the recording sheet, note the total number of errors to the point where the student stopped, and the number of omissions and substitutions made.
3. Note the sentence in which they have made four or more errors. This is the students' frustration level. Instructional level will be one grade level lower. (e.g. frustration level was 3rd grade thus instructional level will be 2nd).
4. Using only <u>UNDERLINED</u> words, calculate Accuracy Rate:

<u># Of Correct Underlined Words X 100</u> = % of correct words read
Total Underlined Words read (in passage)
EXAMPLE: <u>42 X 100</u> = 42% accuracy rate
                100

Assessing Prosody

Use the following qualitative rubric*

Score	Description
0	Segmenting words with no blending of sounds e.g. /m/ /a/ /t/.
1	Reads single words, no "flow" Telegraphic like in sound. No attention to punctuation.
2	Some phrasing is noted (2-3 words at a time), no attention to punctuation.
3	Pauses for ending punctuation, inflection changes may not be always present.
4	Appropriate "flow" and phrasing is noted as well as attention to punctuation with pauses and appropriate inflection most of the time.
5	Reading generally flows. Voice changes, reflect meaning changes. Appropriate ending inflections. All consistently throughout the text.

* adapted from: Tindal, G. & Marston, D. (1996). Technical adequacy of alternative reading measures as performance assessments. *Exceptionality,* 6, 201-230.

The Good Dog

That dog is little and red. He is my pal. I call him Spot. Spot likes to play at my house, but then he runs away to his home up the hill.

Every day the children, who live around here, ask to see Spot. They think the dog is funny when he sprints past them to the plants and drops the stick that they tossed. On most days we all romp in the grass with Spot from sun-up to sunset.

Graduated Running Recording Sheet: Pre-primer / Primer Level

Student:_____ Teacher:_____ School: Date:_____

Words Correct_____ **Total Words** _____ **Total time**_____

Self-Corrections_____ **Omissions**_____ **Substitutions**__

End Sentence_____ **% Accuracy**_____ **Prosody**_____

Retell Score_____

Pre-primer:

The Good Dog   **Notes**

That dog is little and red. He$_5$ is my pal.

I call him Spot$_{10}$. Spot likes to play at my house,

but$_{15}$ then he runs away to his home$_{20}$ up the hill.

Primer:

Every day$_{25}$ the children, who live around

here, ask to see Spot. They think$_{30}$ the dog is funny

when he sprints past them to the plants$_{35}$ and drops

the stick that they tossed. On most days we all romp$_{40}$

in the grass with Spot from sun-up to sunset$_{45}$.

Retell

That **dog** is **little and red**.	1.
He is **my pal**.	2.
I call him **Spot**.	3.
Spot **likes to play** at my house, but then he **runs away** to **his home** up the hill.	4.
Every day the children, **who live around here**, ask to **see Spot**.	5.
They think the **dog is funny** when he **sprints past.**	6.
them **to the plants** and **drops the stick** that they tossed.	
On most days we all romp in the grass with Spot from sun-up to sunset.	7.

Retell
Score:

First Home

What made this a good place for a mother, father, and children to work and play? Many children who were living on this land a very long time ago slept at night in little huts. These small houses were made with reeds or branches and had places carefully made of stones for cooking the food the family found. Early each morning the hard-working people living together in the tiny village were ready to walk to different places looking for special foods. After gathering a variety of edible acorns and seeds using woven reed baskets, these women and girls of the settlement mashed their mounds of nuts into meal. Several men traveling by particular routes into the wilderness hunted the plentiful small prey such as squirrels, rabbits, and birds with nets, curved throwing sticks, or bows and arrows. Other adults rowed large wooden boats protected with tar to neighboring island settlements to trade for unique and nourishing sources of protein to expand their seafood diet.

Graduated Running Record Recording Sheet - Form A

Student:_____ Teacher:_____ School:_____Date:_____

Words Correct_____ Total Words _____ Total time_____

Self-Corrections_____ Omissions_____ Substitutions_____

End Sentence_____ % Accuracy_____ Prosody_____

Retell Score_____

First Home

What made this a good place$_5$ for a mother, father, and children to work$_{10}$ and play? *Mid 1st*

Many children who were living on this land$_{15}$ a very long time ago slept at night in little huts$_{20}$. *End 1st*

These small houses were made with reeds or branches and had places carefully$_{25}$ made of stones for cooking the food the family found. *End 2nd*

Early$_{30}$ each morning the hard-working people living together$_{35}$ in the tiny village were ready to walk to different places looking for special$_{40}$ foods. *End 3rd*

After gathering a variety of edible acorns and seeds using$_{45}$ woven reed baskets, these women and girls of the settlement mashed$_{50}$ their mounds of nuts into meal. *End 4th*

Several men traveling by particular$_{55}$ routes into the wilderness hunted the plentiful small prey such as squirrels$_{60}$, rabbits, and birds with nets, curved throwing sticks, or bows and arrows$_{65}$. *End 5th*

Other adults rowed large wooden boats protected with tar to neighboring$_{70}$ island settlements to trade for unique and nourishing sources of protein$_{75}$ to expand their seafood diet$_{78}$. *End 6th*

Graduated Running Record Retell Form A

Name:_____ Teacher:_____ School:_____

First Home	**Retell:**
What made this a **good place** for a **mother, father, and children** to **work and play**?	1.
Many children who were living on this land a very **long time ago slept** at night **in little huts**.	2.
These small **houses** were **made with reeds or branches** and had places carefully made of **stones for cooking** the food the family found.	3.
Early each morning the **hard-working people** living together **in the tiny village** were ready to **walk** to different places **looking for special foods**.	4.
After gathering a variety of edible **acorns and seeds** using woven reed **baskets**, these **women and girls** of the settlement **mashed their mounds of nuts** into meal.	5.
Several **men** traveling by particular routes **into the wilderness hunted** the plentiful small prey such as **squirrels, rabbits, and birds** with **nets, curved throwing sticks, or bows and arrows**.	6.
Other **adults rowed large wooden boats** protected with tar **to neighboring island** settlements **to trade** for unique and nourishing **sources of protein** to expand their seafood diet.	7.

Retell
Score:

Making Work Like Play

That man comes to this place to work and to play with his children. He thinks it's great to swim under the water to find many animals that live there. This morning he quietly noticed some light green fish eating insects that carefully landed on the blue water near the beach. As the seaside became more crowded, he swam to the entrance of another cove because he knew there would be hundreds of limpets covering the rough rocks along the shore. Here on the island's windward side, the ocean waves entered the cove's coral-guarded boundaries without a problem and then fought to escape to the freedom of the open sea again. From all indications, the shoreline explorer was convinced he would be astonished by the impressive number of oysters and other sea creatures living in the cove free from threatening pollution. In his role as a prominent marine biologist, he planned to conduct extensive research on the organisms found in this watery environment while vowing to protect it aggressively from inappropriate use by hostile commercial businesses.

Graduated Running Recording Sheet - Form B

Student:_____Teacher:_____School:_____Date:_____

Words Correct_____ Total Words _____ Total time_____

Self-Corrections_____ Omissions_____ Substitutions_____

End Sentence_____ % Accuracy_____ Prosody_____

Retell Score_____

Making Work Like Play

That man comes to this$_5$ place to work and to play with his children.$_{10}$ Mid 1st

He thinks it's great to swim under the water$_{15}$ to find many animals that live there.$_{20}$. End 1st

This morning he quietly noticed some light$_{25}$ green fish eating insects that carefully$_{30}$ landed on the blue water near the beach. End 2nd

As the seaside$_{35}$ became more crowded, he swam to the entrance of another$_{40}$ cove because he knew there would be hundreds of limpets$_{45}$ covering the rough rocks along the shore. End 3rd

Here on the island's$_{50}$ windward side, the ocean waves entered the cove's coral-guarded$_{55}$ boundaries without a problem and then fought to escape to the freedom$_{60}$ of the open sea again. End 4th

From all indications, the shoreline explorer was convinced$_{65}$ he would be astonished by the impressive number of oysters and other sea creatures$_{70}$ living in the cove free from threatening pollution. End 5th

In his role as a prominent marine biologist$_{75}$, he planned to conduct extensive research on the organisms$_{80}$ found in this watery environment while vowing to protect$_{85}$ it aggressively from inappropriate use by hostile commercial businesses$_{90}$. End 6th

Graduated Running Retell Form B

Name:_____ Teacher:_____ School:_____

Making Work Like Play

That **man** comes to this place **to work** and **to play with his children.**

1.

He thinks **it's great** to **swim under the water** to **find many animals** that live there.

2.

This morning he quietly **noticed some light green fish eating insects** that carefully landed on the blue water **near the beach**.

3.

As the seaside became **more crowded**, he swam to the entrance of **another cove** because he knew there would be **hundreds of limpets** covering the rough rocks **along the shore**.

4.

Here on the island's **windward side**, the ocean waves entered **the cove's coral-guarded boundaries** without a problem and then **fought to escape** to the freedom of **the open sea again**.

5.

From all indications, the **shoreline explorer** was convinced he **would be astonished** by the impressive **number of oysters and other sea creatures** living in **the cove** free from **threatening pollution**.

6.

In his role as a prominent **marine biologist**, he planned to **conduct extensive research** on the **organisms found** in this watery environment while **vowing to protect** it aggressively from **inappropriate use** by hostile commercial **businesses.**

7.

Retell
Score:

The Interactive Reading Assessment System – Revised

Introduction and Overview

The Interactive Reading Assessment System – Revised (IRAS-R) is an informal reading inventory comprised of a set of subtests that is individually administered to determine a student's reading strengths and weaknesses. The skills tested include most of those generally accepted as necessary for success in skilled reading. The rationale for the array of tasks selected for IRAS-R rests on a theory of reading as a set of independent component skills (Calfee & Drum, 1979). By "independent" we mean that a student may have relative strengths or weaknesses within the several areas. The primary skill areas reflected in the tasks include decoding, vocabulary, grammar, understanding paragraphs and understanding longer passages (Calfee & Spector, 1981).

IRAS is particularly suited to students past the initial primer level. The materials in the test are selected to cover a wide range of skills and knowledge in the areas of reading and oral language, from the level expected of a midyear first grader to that of a junior high school student.

If all subtests of the IRAS are selected, IRAS can be administered in one session of about 40 to 50 minutes, or in two sessions of approximately 30 minutes each. However, the system is designed to assess one or more skills as needed, a selection of appropriate subtests should be made to address the identified skills in question. If you are planning to administer the sight word and the comprehension tasks, use the word recognition/decoding first. Directions for administration are included at the beginning of each subtest.

Decoding and word knowledge is measured in four ways. First, students are asked to read common sight words within the student's reading vocabulary and beyond. Next, the student is asked to define words. Depending on how well he or she performs, the student is moved to lists of easier or more difficult words. Then, letter-sound correspondence is measured in two ways using an alphabet recognition task that asks for letter identification and letter-sound relationships and by having the student read lists of synthetic words. The synthetic words are divided into six categories according to the spelling pattern: vowels controlled by a final "e", vowels controlled by single and double consonants, vowel and consonant digraphs, vowel plus "r", segmented polysyllables, and polysyllabic words the student is asked to divide before reading. Finally, the student is asked to spell or build a list of phonetically regular synthetic words of increasing difficulty.

Oral reading and comprehension is assessed in several ways. The sentence reading and text passages roughly correspond to the sight word reading lists. First, the student is asked to read a graded series of sentences to assess fluency. The next sets of tasks includes reading narrative and expository passages to assess comprehension. The materials are designed to give students the opportunity to read orally and silently. Passages above students' reading ability are also included to assess students' listening comprehension. Comprehension is assessed with a retelling of the passage and answering probe questions.

Interactive Reading Assessment System Summary Page

Student: _____ Teacher: _____ Grade: _____

Administrator: _____School: _____ Date: _____

Age: _____ Circle one: Male Female

First Language: English Spanish Other Specify: _____

	Raw Score	Grade Level
Alphabet Recognition: **# named** **# sounds known**		
Word Recognition / Decoding: Last list passed		
Meta-Linguistic Question: Rubric score		
Vocabulary: Last list passed		
Letter-Sound Correspondence **(synthetic words):** Last list passed		
Building synthetic words:_____ # built		
Sentence Reading: Last sentence passed		
Reading Fluency		
Reading Comprehension		

Notes:_____
_____
_____
_____
_____
_____
_____

Alphabet Recognition:

Directions: Tester points to a letter, and says, "What is the name of this letter? What sound does it make?"

a   s   m   u   e   n

c   p   l   o   t   d

A   S   M   U   E   N

C   P   L   O   T   D

Decoding and Vocabulary Response Sheet

Directions:

I. Word Recognition / Decoding:

Show the first four lists to the student and ask which list is the most difficult one he/she can read. Begin with that list. Proceed through the lists until **4 or more errors** are made on one list. If 4 errors are made on the first list attempted, have the student try the previous list. Continue in this fashion until three or less errors are made. Once you have established the word recognition level proceed to Step II. Meta-Language.

II. Meta-Language:

Select the last word pronounced correctly. Ask the meta-language question:

"You were right when you said _____ for this word. How did you know to pronounce

(say) it that way?"

If the student is reluctant to answer, use probes such as:

"Have you seen that word **before?" "Did it remind you of another word?" Do these letters or syllables help you? How?.**

III. Vocabulary:

Beginning with the decoding list on which the student failed, tell the student the first underlined word and ask for the definition. If the student is unable to define the word, use the accompanying prompt and place a check on the prompt line. Record the student's responses. Continue asking for the definitions of only the underlined words until the student is unable to define two underlined words on one list. If the student is unable to define the first word set attempted go back through the lists until the student is able to define at least two words.

Word List	Decoding	Prompt	Definition/Alternatives

X   Grade Level: Early 1st

mud _____ _____
                                        a large wet bird, wet dirt, a book

pig _____ _____

its _____ _____

glad _____ _____
                                        sad, nervous, happy

sent _____ _____

top _____ _____
                                        A high place, inside a box, bottom

Y   Grade Level: Early 1st

spent _____ _____

rub _____ _____
                                        To wash, to brush together, to bounce

basket _____ _____
                                        Something to hold things, to bounce, to drive

until _____ _____

them _____ _____

mist _____ _____
                                        A light rain, a shaggy dog, a window

- Use only when the last correct list is reached.
- Select the hardest word pronounce correctly.

"You were right when you said _____ for this word. How did you know to

pronounce (say) it that way?"_____

_____

A. Grade Level: Mid 1st

end	v	_____	_____	_____
				to: stop, go slow, start
long		_____		
little	a.	_____	_____	_____
				something: large, tall, small
time		_____		
house	n.	_____	_____	_____
				animal to ride, place to live, bus stop
same		_____		

B. Grade Level: Late 1st

food	n.	_____	_____	_____
				something: to eat, to wear, to play
city		_____		
best	a.	_____	_____	_____
				something: as sweet as can be, as big as can be, as good as can be
paper		_____		
tell	v.	_____	_____	_____
				to: cry, say, yell
room		_____		

- Use only when the last correct list is reached.
- Select the hardest word pronounce correctly.

"You were right when you said _____ for this word. How did you know to

pronounce (say) it that way?"_____

_____

C. Grade Level: Mid 2nd

<u>fast</u>   a.   _____   _____

quick, loud, slow

black   _____

<u>feel</u>   v.   _____   _____

to: tease, taste, touch

table   _____

<u>birds</u>   n.   _____   _____

thorns on a bush, animals with feathers, animals with scales

cold   _____

D. Grade Level: End 2nd

<u>music</u>   n.   _____   _____

sound patterns, loud noises, twinkling lights

watch   _____

<u>explain</u>   v.   _____   _____

to: tell your name, count to ten, tell meaning

color   _____

<u>heat</u>   v.   _____   _____

to: burn, warm, go fast

machine   _____

- Use only when the last correct list is reached.
- Select the hardest word pronounce correctly.

"You were right when you said _____ for this word. How did you know to

pronounce (say) it that way?"_____

_____

E. Grade Level: Mid 3rd

skin   n.   _____ _____
                                                    _____
                                                    outside of a balloon, outside
                                                    of your body, inside of a
race   _____   grape

afraid   a.   _____ _____
                                                    _____
                                                    surprised, frightened,
please   _____   successful

fight   v.   _____ _____
                                                    _____
middle   _____   to: hit, break, fall

F. Grade Level: End 3rd

hungry   a.   _____ _____
                                                    _____
                                                    in a hurry, going away,
finger   _____   wanting food

visit   v.   _____ _____
                                                    _____
                                                    to go: to see a friend, for a
electric   _____   bus ride, to a show

crowd   n.   _____ _____
                                                    _____
                                                    kind of party, type of bird, lots of
kitchen   _____   people

- Use only when the last correct list is reached.
- Select the hardest word pronounce correctly.

"You were right when you said _____ for this word. How did you know to

pronounce (say) it that way?"_____

_____

G. Grade Level: Mid 4th

lonely   a.   _____   _____   _____
                                                                                to: want friends, feel sad, wait for dinner

development   _____

ability   n.   _____   _____   _____
                                                                                    a kind of: test, skill, award

honor   _____

observe   v.   _____   _____   _____
                                                                                   to: see through, look at, light up

industry   _____

H. Grade Level: End 4th

committee   n.   _____   _____   _____
                                                                                    people who: meet, have a party, build a house

atom   _____

delicate   a.   _____   _____   _____
                                                                                   breakable, soft, round

judge   _____

prevent   v.   _____   _____   _____
                                                                                    to: stop, allow, pretend

mission   _____

- Use only when the last correct list is reached.
- Select the hardest word pronounce correctly.

"You were right when you said _____ for this word. How did you know to pronounce (say) it that way?"_____

_____

I. Grade Level: Mid 5th

issue   v.   _____   _____

                                                     to: order, give, refuse

muscle   _____

annual   a.   _____   _____

                                                     lately, monthly, yearly

curiosity   _____

literature   v.   _____   _____

                                                     kinds of writing, bag of trash,
scratch paper

permanent   _____

J. Grade Level: End 5th

decade   n.   _____   _____

                                                       several days, ten years, two
weeks

bomb   _____

promptly   adv.   _____   _____

                                                     helpfully, in a hurry, right
away

grease   _____

demonstrate v.   _____   _____

                                                     to: experiment, demand, show

extensive   _____

- Use only when the last correct list is reached.
- Select the hardest word pronounce correctly.

"You were right when you said _____ for this word. How did you know to

pronounce (say) it that way?"_____

_____

K. Grade Level: Mid 6th

deserve   v.   _____ _____ _____
to have the: need, wish, right

retain   _____

consequence n.   _____ _____ _____
outcome, failure, lie

graduation   _____

ominous   a.   _____ _____ _____
threatening, shocking, appealing

skyscraper   _____

L. Grade Level: End 6th

proclaim   v.   _____ _____ _____
to: shout, deny, announce

elegance   _____

controversial a.   _____ _____ _____
agreeable, debatable,
doubtful

astute   _____

aroma   n.   _____ _____ _____
pleasant smell, pretty sunset,
spicy taste

implement   _____

- Use only when the last correct list is reached.
- Select the hardest word pronounce correctly.

"You were right when you said _____ for this word. How did you know to

pronounce (say) it that way?"_____

_____

M. Grade Level: Mid 7th

pessimistic   a.   _____   _____   _____

dormant   _____   gloomy, worried, happy

boredom   n.   _____   _____   _____
                                                           drowsiness, activity, monotony

prudent   _____

illuminate   v.   _____   _____   _____

frustration   _____   to: burn, light up, destroy

N. Grade Level: End 7th

mandatory a.   _____   _____   _____

flamboyant   _____   required, permitted, released

traverse   v.   _____   _____   _____
                                                           to: jump on, go across, stand up

veritable   _____

anthology   n.   _____   _____   _____
                                                           collection of stories, study of man, humorous saying

tumultuous   _____

- Use only when the last correct list is reached.
- Select the hardest word pronounce correctly.

"You were right when you said _____ for this word. How did you know to pronounce (say) it that way?"_____

_____

Decoding Synthetic Words Lists:

Directions: Stop at four or more errors in one list and ask the metacognitive question at the bottom of the page. (List E is read as blended words. Words in List F are read first as separate syllables and then blended.)

Word List A

hin _____

nelp _____

flass _____

scrong _____

pame _____

vute _____

Word List B

shile _____

throve _____

snay _____

toin _____

spawk _____

spleek _____

Word List C

clur _____

derb _____

folp _____

sark _____

shald _____

plair _____

Word List D

worch _____

knop _____

ceft _____

flage _____

wrudge _____

glies _____

Word List E

lod-ded _____

fen-ing _____

wem-bick _____

lude-ful _____

un-fro-ten _____

im-pen-tive _____

af-fre-mi-a-tion _____

syn-thod _____

an-a-phen-ist _____

Word List F

jemming _____

saped _____

rimple _____

befade _____

dacture _____

conspartable _____

rhosmic _____

paraplast _____

euchormonium _____

Metacognition:

"You were right when you said_____ for this word. How did you know to pronounce (say) it that way?" _____

_____

Possible prompts: Have you seen the word before? Did it remind you of another word?

Word Building: Synthetic Words

       If available lay out the appropriate letter tiles for student word building activities. If letter tiles are not available use pencil and paper.

"Now, I'm going to say some funny pretend words and I want you to say the word after me. Then I want you to build the word for me." If the student misspells the word, continue through the set of three until a word is spelled correctly. If none are spelled correctly, stop.

A.
1. dut (but) _____

2. mape (cape) _____

3. leb (web) _____

B.
4. fening (screening) _____

5. sidded (bid..) _____

6. javes (caves) _____

C.
7. broint (joint) _____

8. glire (fire) _____

9. grotious (ferocious) _____

D.
10. frintle (mint..) _____

11. choober (goober) _____

12. pridder (grider) _____

E.
13. strandister (stand..sister) _____

14. closterish (roster..wish) _____

15. thrinkerlant (thinker..land) _____

Metacognition:

"You were right when you spelled this word _____. How did you know to spell it that way?_____

_____

_____

Student:_____ Date:_____ Score:_____

School:_____ Teacher:_____

Directions: Stop when the student fails to read a minimum of **one highlighted** word correctly or when student takes more than 20 seconds to read. Score 1 point for each completed sentence, _ point for partial success (only one word read correctly).

A. I **LIKE** to **PLAY**.
    I like to eat a **RED** apple.

B. Ann wants Mom to **MAKE** a **CAKE**. Mom cannot do it. She has to go to **WORK**.

C. The man made the light **SHINE**. Right away Ed saw the baby **FOX** on top of its **CAGE**.

D. The kitten was **SCARED** and climbed up the tree. The girl tried to **REACH** it but she had no **LUCK**.

E. Jeff was **AFRAID** that he would miss the first act. As soon as he bought the **POPCORN**, he **HURRIED** to find Rose.

F. About three miles from the **HARBOR**, Ray's boat was **CAUGHT** in an unexpected **CURRENT**.

G. Harriet made many heroic **ATTEMPTS** to lead other slaves to freedom in the North. Her courage and **DETERMINATION** made her an **IMPORTANT** figure in the nation's history.

H. Slowly the women **ASCENDED** the steep and icy **MOUNTAIN**. There were times when the sheer cliffs and the bitter cold **DISCOURAGED** them, but they would not relent.

Passage Reading Introduction and Directions

(Note: Due to space constraints, we have included 1st, 3rd, and 6th grade samples of the Passage Reading Subtest. The complete set of passages and recording sheets can be accessed at this website: education.ucr.edu/read_plus. After studying the IRAS Passage Reading format, teachers are encouraged to create similar grade level passages with retelling and probe recording sheets from materials in the level book sets typically found in today's classrooms.

First, the student enters the passage reading subtest at the starting point indicated by his Sentence Reading performance. If the student reads the sentence set at Level C with adequate speed and accuracy, but cannot meet these criteria for Level D, then he should begin with Oral Reading Comprehension, Narrative C 1.

The student begins with either the Oral or Silent Reading task, depending on his entering level. If he cannot read Sentence Set X or A, or if he failed Word List A, then he should go immediately to Listening Comprehension, Narrative A2.

At each passage level, the student is tested on the narrative passage first, then the expository passage at the same level. Most students will find the narrative structure easier to comprehend than the expository structure.

<u>Stop Rules</u>:

For oral reading, the task is ended whenever the student exceeds 100 seconds to read a passage. Time is the only criterion; comprehension is <u>not</u> taken into account.

For silent reading and listening:

1. The student has succeeded at the retelling task if he passes half or more of the designated items.

2. The student has passed an element if he at least mentions it briefly.

The guiding principle in this task, as elsewhere in IRAS, is to give the student the benefit of the doubt and move onward to a more difficult task whenever possible.

		Response		Probe Questions
		Retell	Probe	
Setting	It is a sunny day. ANN is on her bike.	_____		
1.				
Goal	TOM WANTS to PLAY BALL	_____		
Attempt	He ASKS ANN to PLAY with him	_____	_____	What did Tom want Ann to do?
2.				
Outcome Initiating event	She will NOT PLAY ball now She WANTS to RIDE	_____	_____	What did Ann want to do (. . . when Tom asked her to play?)
Reaction	TOM is SAD	_____		
3.				
Attempt	He ASKS Ann, "Can we take a RIDE and THEN PLAY BALL?	_____	_____	What did Tom say to Ann? (. . . when she didn't want to play ball)
4.				
Outcome	"YES" SAYS ANN. "That will be fun"	_____		
Resolution	So TOM GETS his BIKE and THEY PLAY	_____	_____	How did story end?

TIME STOP _____

Oral Reading

Comprehension/Nar A1

		Response		Probe Questions
		Retell	Probe	
Setting	JILL HAS a TREE HOUSE	_____		
1.				
Goal	She WANTS to PAINT IT green	_____		
Attempt	She ASKS SAM to HELP	_____	_____	What did Jill want Sam to do?
2.				
Outcome Initiating event	SAM CANNOT help He is GOING OUT with Pat	_____ _____	_____	What was Sam going to do? (. . .when Jill asked him to help)
Reaction	JILL is SAD	_____		
3.				
Attempt	She ASKS DAD, "CAN YOU come out and HELP me?"	_____	_____	What did Jill ask Dad?
4.				
Outcome	"YES," SAYS DAD. "I will help you paint the tree house."	_____		
Resolution	So JILL goes to GET the green PAINT	_____	_____	How did the story end?

Comprehension/Nar A2

Listening

36

		Retell	Probe	Probe Questions
Setting	Once there was an old MAN who LIVED BY a RIVER. It was WINTER and the RIVER was COVERED with ICE	_____		

1.

Initiating event	One day he looked out his window and SAW a BOY by the river. The boy started to WALK ACROSS the river on the ICE	_____	_____	What were the man and the boy doing at the beginning of story?
Reaction	The old MAN was AFRAID that the ICE would BREAK	_____		

2.

Attempt	He opened the window and CALLED out to the boy	_____		
Outcome	But the BOY DIDN'T HEAR him, and he just KEPT on GOING	_____	_____	What happened when the old man saw the boy walk on the ice? (What did the man do?) (What did the boy do?)

3.

Initiating event	When he got to the middle the ICE BROKE, and the BOY FELL into the WATER	_____	_____	What happened when the boy got to the middle of the river?

4.

Attempt	The old MAN GOT a long LADDER and ran down to the river. He SLID the ladder ACROSS the ICE.	_____	_____	What did the man do when the boy feel in?

5.

Outcome	The BOY GRABBED the LADDER and the MAN PULLED him OUT	_____	_____	How was the boy saved?

6.

Resolution	The next day the BOY visited the old man and THANKED him for saving his life	_____	_____	How did story end?

TIME STOP

_____

Oral Reading

Comprehension/Nar C1

		Response		
		<u>Retell</u>	<u>Probe</u>	<u>Probe Questions</u>
1.	One way to MAKE MONEY in the summer is to SELL LEMONADE	_____	_____	How can you make money in the summer?
2.	It is easy to make. You NEED LEMONS, WATER, SUGAR, and ICE.	_____	_____	What do you need to make lemonade?
3.	PUT the JUICE from TEN LEMONS into TEN CUPS of WATER. ADD TWO CUPS of SUGAR and lots of ICE. Then stir it.	_____	_____	How do you make lemonade?
4.	When you have the lemonade GET some PAPER CUPS and enough MONEY to make CHANGE. Also get a SMALL TABLE to put things on.	_____	_____	What things do you need to get beside lemonade?
5.	The FIND a SPOT to set up. The CORNER of a STREET is GOOD.	_____	_____	Where is a good spot to set up your table?
6.	When it GETS HOT, PEOPLE will stop to BUY a DRINK.	_____	_____	When will people stop to buy a drink?

Listening

Comprehension/Exp C2

		Response		
		Retell	Probe	Probe Questions
Setting	Once there was a little GIRL who HAD a KITTEN. The KITTEN liked to PLAY in the YARD by a tall tree	_____		
1. Initiating event	Early one morning a dog was walking in front of the house. It was windy and the gate blew open. The DOG RAN INTO the YARD. The KITTEN was SCARED and RAN UP the TREE.	_____	_____	What happened at the beginning of the story?
2. Attempt	The GIRL TRIED to REACH it, but	_____	_____	What happened when the kitten ran up the tree?
Outcome	She had NO LUCK. The KITTEN CLIMBED to the HIGHEST BRANCH	_____	_____	(what happened when the girl tried to reach the kitten?)
3. Initiating event	The girl's SISTER SAW the kitten FROM her WINDOW	_____	_____	What did the girl's sister see?
4. Attempt	She OPENED the window and LEANED OUT. She COULD REACH the BRANCH. "COME INSIDE," she SAID softly.	_____	_____	How did the sister try to save the kitten?
5. Outcome	She REACHED out when the KITTEN came closer. The she PULLED it INTO the HOUSE	_____	_____	What happened when the kitten came near the window?
6. Resolution	The night the little GIRL TOLD everyone WHAT HAPPENED. She was GLAD that her SISTER had SAVED the KITTEN	_____	_____	How did story end?

Listening

Comprehension/Nar C2

39

Response

Retell   Probe   Probe Questions

1.

It is easy to MAKE BUTTER. First you   _____   _____   What do you need to
NEED a JAR and some heavy   make butter?
CREAM.

2.

FILL the JAR PART way with   _____   _____   What is the first thing
CREAM. Then SHAKE it for about 20   you do?
MINUTES.

3.

SOON the CREAM will start to get   _____   _____   When should you stop
LUMPY. STOP WHEN most of the   shaking the cream?
cream turns into LUMPS. You will find
that the LUMPS are BUTTER.

4.

Take the lumps out of the jar and   _____   _____   What do you do with
WASH them with COLD WATER.   the lumps in the jar?

5.

Mix a little SALT with the lumps of   _____   _____   After you wash the
butter and PAT them TOGETHER.   butter, what do you
Leave the butter in a COOL PLACE   do?
over night.

6.

In the morning the BUTTER will be   _____   _____   How do you know
HARD and READY to EAT.   when the butter is
                                                               ready to eat?

TIME STOP

_____

Oral Reading

Comprehension/Exp C1

		Response		
		Retell	Probe	Probe Questions
Setting	It was the year <u>1849</u> in the small town of BUCKSTOWN, MARYLAND	_____		
1.				
Goal	A Young, black SLAVE, named Harriet Tubman, DECIDED to ESCAPE from the SOUTH and SEEK her FREEDOM. Harriet AWAITED a CHANCE to begin the trip NORTHWARD.	_____	_____	What did Harriet want to do at beginning?
2.				
Initiating event	One evening a farmer VOLUNTEERED to HIDE Harriet in his CART underneath a LOAD of VEGETABLES.	_____	_____	How did the farmer help Harriet?
Reaction	Harriet was TERRIFIED that she would be CAUGHT trying to escape, but she was DETERMINED to take the RISK.			
3.				
Attempt	Harriet TRAVELED on a ROUTE known as the UNDERGROUND RAILROAD. The underground was not a real railroad, but an ORGANIZATION of people who PROVIDED rides and hiding places for slaves ESCAPING from PLANTATIONS in the South.	_____	_____	What route did Harriet travel?
4.				
Elaboration (definition)		———	———	What was the underground railroad?
5.				
Outcome	Harriet spent several exhausting NIGHTS traveling. Finally she ARRIVED at the PENNSYLVANIA border. She was a FREE citizen for the first time in her life.	_____	_____	Tell about Harriet's trip. (How did it end?)
6.				
Resolution	AFTERWARD, Harriet made many HEROIC ATTEMPTS to LEAD other SLAVES to FREEDOM in the North. Because of her COURAGE and DETERMINATION she is an important FIGURE in the NATION'S HISTORY.	_____	_____	Why is Harriet an important figure in the nation's history?

Silent Reading

Comprehension/Nar F1

		Response		
		<u>Retell</u>	<u>Probe</u>	<u>Probe Questions</u>
Setting	It was WINTER in the town of KITTY HAWK, NORTH CAROLINA	_____		
1.				
Goal	This was the day WILBUR and ORVILLE WRIGHT PLANNED their attempt to BECOME the FIRST men to FLY in an ENGINE-POWERED AIRPLANE.	_____	_____	What did Wilbur and Orville plan to do?
2.				
Initiating event	When the two men AROSE at DAWN, the WIND was BRISK and a THREAT of RAIN lingered in the air	_____	_____	What was the weather like the day of the flight?
3.				
Elaboration (description)	The DECISION they had to make was DIFFICULT. It might be DANGEROUS to fly in high WINDS, especially IF they ENCOUNTERED a SUDDEN GUST. But if the WIND held steady, it COULD actually HELP them in TAKING OFF.	_____	_____	Why was their decision difficult?
Reaction	WILBUR and ORVILLE were NERVOUS as they made their historic decision.	_____		
4.				
Attempt	At about NOON, they STARTED the ENGINE. Suspense mounted as the AIRPLANE MOVED forward and gradually LIFTED into the air.	_____	_____	What happened about noon that day?
5.				
Outcome	The machine FLEW for a brief TWELVE SECONDS before COMING to a HALT on the ground.	_____	_____	How did the flight turn out? How long did they fly?
6.				
Resolution	Wilbur and Orville were TRIUMPHANT. They had accomplished their goal. Their achievement that day marked the BEGINNING of man's VENTURE INTO the SKY.	_____	_____	Why was their achievement important?

Listening

Comprehension/Nar F2

		Retell	Probe	Probe Questions

1. You can still FIND GOLD in some California streams. All you NEED is a METAL PAN and a lot of LUCK.

   Retell _____ Probe _____

   What do you need to pan for gold?

2. First SELECT a place where the CURRENT is SLOW. GOLD is CARRIED BY moving WATER, but DROPS to the stream bed WHERE the WATER is STILL.

   _____ _____

   What is the first thing you should do? (Why is it best to pan where the water is still?)

3. Next SCOOP some GRAVEL from the stream INTO your PAN and gently WASH OUT and DIRT.

   _____ _____

   What is the first thing you do with your scoop of gravel?

4. Then PUT a little WATER in the PAN and ROCK it in a circle so that the larger bits of GRAVEL will SPILL OUT.

   _____ _____

   What do you do when the dirt is washed out?

5. Soon there should be only a HANDFUL of SAND LEFT. LOOK for SHINY YELLOW PARTICLES.

   _____ _____

   What is left when the gravel spills out of the pan?

6. You can DETERMINE if these are GOLD by HITTING them WITH a HAMMER. Real GOLD will FLATTEN BECAUSE it is SOFT.

   _____ _____

   How can you tell if the shiny particles are gold?

Silent Reading

Comprehension/Exp F1

Probe Questions

1.   A CATERPILLAR makes a sleeping bag   _____   _____   What is the cocoon
         called a COCOON. It USES a kind of   made of?
         STICKY THREAD that comes from its
         mouth.

2.   First the caterpillar GRABS a TWIG with   _____   _____   What is first thing the
         its BACK FEET. This leaves the front part   caterpillar does? (How
         of its body free to move.   does it grab the twig?)

3.   Then it begins to BEND and TURN and   _____   _____   What   does   the
         SPIN the THREAD around itself and the   caterpillar do after it
         twig like a net. But it leaves room inside   grabs the twig?
         the net to move around.

4.   When the net is made the caterpillar   _____   _____   What happens after the
         MOVES its HEAD back and forth to PUT   net is made?
         in a FLOOR.

5.   Then it FILLS in all the SPACES in the net _____   _____   What does it do after it
         and finally CLOSES it all up.   puts in the floor?

6.   After that the caterpillar goes to SLEEP. _____   _____   What happens after the
         When it WAKES up in a few months it   net is finally closed?
         will be a MOTH.

Listening

Comprehension/Exp F2

Interactive Reading Assessment System (IRIS-R) Student Pages

Developed by

Robert C. Calfee

University of California, Riverside

Kathryn Hoover Calfee

Palo Alto Unified School District

a   s   m   u   e   n

c   p   l   o   t   d

Alphabet Recognition

A   S   M   U   E   N

C   P   L   O   T   D

Alphabet Recognition

X	Y
mud	spent
pig	rub
its	basket
glad	until
sent	them
top	mist

A

end

long

little

time

house

same

B

food

city

best

paper

tell

room

C

fast

black

feel

table

birds

cold

D

music

watch

explain

color

heat

machine

Decoding/Vocabulary

E

skin

race

afraid

please

fight

middle

F

hungry

finger

visit

electric

crowd

kitchen

G

lonely

development

ability

honor

observe

industry

H

committee

atom

delicate

judge

prevent

mission

Decoding/Vocabulary

I

issue

muscle

annual

curiosity

literature

permanent

J

decade

bomb

promptly

grease

demonstrate

extensive

K

deserve

retain

consequence

graduation

ominous

skyscraper

L

proclaim

elegance

controversial

astute

aroma

implement

Decoding/Vocabulary

M	N
pessimistic	mandatory
dormant	flamboyant
boredom	traverse
prudent	veritable
illuminate	anthology
frustration	tumultuous

List 1	List 2
hin	shile
nelp	throve
flass	snay
scrong	toin
pame	spawk
vute	spleek

Letter Sound Correspondence

List 3	List 4
clur	worch
derb	knop
folp	ceft
sark	flage
shald	wruge
plair	glies

Letter Sound Correspondence

List 5	List 6
lod - ded	jemming
fen - ing	saped
wem - bick	rimple
lude - ful	befade
un - fro - ten	dacture
im - pen - tive	rhosmic
af - fre - mi - a - tion	conspartable
syn - thod	rhosmic
an - a - phen - ist	paraplast
	euchormonium

Letter Sound Correspondences

X. I like to play.

I like to eat a red apple.

A. Mom cannot do it. She has to go to work.

B. The man made the light shine. Right away Ed saw the baby fox on top of its cage.

C. The kitten was scared and climbed up the tree. The girl tried to reach it but she had no luck.

D. Jeff was afraid that he would miss the first act. As soon as he bought the popcorn, he hurried to find Rose.

E. About three miles from the harbor, Ray's boat was caught in an unexpected current.

F. Harriet made many heroic attempts to lead other slaves to freedom in the North. Her courage and determination made her an important figure in the nation's history.

G. Slowly the women ascended the steep and icy mountain. There were times when the sheer cliffs and the bitter cold discouraged them, but they would not relent.

It is a sunny day. Ann is on her bike.

Tom wants to play ball. He asks Ann to

play with him. She will not play ball

now, she wants to ride.

Tom is sad. He asks Ann, "Can we take

a ride and then play ball?"

"Yes," says Ann. "That will be fun."

So Tom gets his bike and they play.

Oral Reading
Comprehensive/Nar Al

Jill has a tree house. She wants to paint it green.

She asks Sam to help.

Sam cannot help. He is going out with Pat.

Jill is sad. She asks Dad, "Can you come out and help me?"

"Yes," says Dad. "I will help you tree house."

So Jill goes to get the green paint.

Listening
Comprehension/Nar A2

Once there was an old man who lived by a river. It was winter and the river was covered with ice. One day he looked out his window and saw a boy by the river. The boy started to walk across the river on the ice.

The old man was afraid that the ice would break. He opened the window and called out to the boy. But the boy didn't hear him, and he just kept on going. When he got to the middle, the ice broke, and the boy fell into the water.

The old man got a long ladder and ran down to the river. He slid the ladder across the ice. The boy grabbed the ladder and the man pulled him out.

The next day the boy visited the old man and thanked him for saving his life.

Oral Reading
Comprehension/Nar C1

It is easy to make butter. First you need a jar and some heavy cream. Fill the jar part way with cream. Then shake it for about 20 minutes. Soon the cream will start to get lumpy. Stop when most of the cream turns into lumps. You will find that the lumps are butter.

Take the lumps out of the jar and wash them with cold water. Mix a little salt with the lumps and pat them together. Leave the butter in a cool place over night. In the morning the butter will be hard and ready to eat.

Oral Reading
Comprehension/Exp C1

Once there was a little girl who had a kitten. The kitten liked to play in the yard by a tall tree.

Early one morning a dog was walking in front of the house. It was windy and the gate blew open. The dog ran into the yard. The kitten was scared and ran up the tree.

The girl tried to reach it, but she had no luck. The kitten climbed to the highest branch. The girl's sister saw the kitten from her window. She opened the window and leaned out. She could reach the branch. "Come inside," she said softly. She reached out when the kitten came closer. Then she pulled it into the house.

That night the little girl told everyone what had happened. She was glad that her sister had saved the kitten.

Listening
Comprehension/Nar C2

One way to make money in the summer is to sell lemonade. It is easy to make. You need lemons, water, sugar, and ice.

Put the juice from ten lemons into ten cups of water. Add two cups of sugar and lots of ice. Then stir it.

When you have the lemonade, get some paper cups and enough money to make change. Also get a small table to put things on. Then find a spot to set up. The corner of a street is good.

When it gets hot, people will stop to buy a drink.

Listening
Comprehension/Exp C2

It was the year 1849 in the small town of Buckstown, Maryland. A young, black slave, named Harriet Tubman, decided to escape from the South and seek her freedom. Harriet awaited a chance to begin the trip northward.

One evening a farmer volunteered to hide Harriet in his cart underneath a load of vegetables. Harriet was terrified that she would be caught trying to escape, but she was determined to take the risk.

Harriet traveled on a route known as the underground railroad. The underground was not a real railroad, but an organization of people who provided rides and hiding places for slaves escaping from plantations in the South.

Harriet spent several exhausting nights traveling. Finally she arrived at the Pennsylvania border. She was a free citizen for the first time in her life.

Afterward, Harriet made many heroic attempts to lead other slaves to freedom in the North. Because of her courage and determination she is an important figure in the nation's history.

Silent Reading
Comprehension/Nar F1

You can still find gold in some California streams. All you need is a metal pan and a lot of luck.

First select a place where the current is slow. Gold is carried by moving water, but drops to the stream bed where the water is still. Next scoop some gravel from the stream into your pan and gently wash out any dirt. Then put a little water in the pan and rock it in a circle so that the larger bits of gravel will spill out. Soon there should be only a handful of sand left. Look for shiny yellow particles. You can determine if these are gold by hitting them with a hammer. Real gold will flatten because it is soft.

Silent Reading
Comprehension/Exp F1

It was winter in the town of Kitty Hawk, North Carolina. This was the day Wilbur and Orville Wright planned an attempt to become the first men to fly in an engine-powered airplane.

When the two men arose at dawn the wind was brisk and a threat of rain lingered in the air. The decision they had to make was difficult. It might be dangerous to fly in high winds, especially if there were a sudden gust. But if the wind held steady it could actually help them in taking off. Wilbur and Orville were nervous as they made the historic decision.

At about noon, they started the engine. Suspense mounted as the airplane moved forward and gradually lifted into the air. The machine flew for a brief twelve seconds before coming to a halt on the ground.

Wilbur and Orville were triumphant. They had accomplished their goal. Their achievement that day marked the beginning of man's venture into the sky.

Listening
Comprehension/Nar F2

A caterpillar makes a sleeping bag called a cocoon. It uses a kind of sticky thread that comes from its mouth.

First the caterpillar grabs a twig with its back feet. This leaves the front part of its body free to move. Then it begins to bend and turn and spin the thread around itself and the twig like a net. But it leaves room inside the net to move around.

When the net is made, the caterpillar moves its head back and forth to put in a floor. Then it fills in all the spaces in the net and finally closes it all up.

After that, the caterpillar goes to sleep. When it wakes up in a few months, it will be a moth.

Listening
Comprehension/Exp F2

Read-Write Cycle Assessments

Introduction

The Read-Write Cycle Assessments are dynamic assessments designed to determine the best writing a student can do on a given topic. The format used with this assessment is grounded in the tenets of social cognitive learning, closely resembles regular classroom instruction, and reflects the reading-writing connection. Included in the design are pre-writing activities that use cooperative/collaborative instructional strategies to scaffold each student's background knowledge. During the pre-writing activities, students work individually, in pairs or small groups, or as a whole class to pool their knowledge and understanding of the topic. These activities work to 'level the playing field' so that the students are better able to demonstrate their ability to compose text in an academic setting without being hampered by less than adequate topic knowledge. Teachers can get a clearer understanding of their students' skill in expressing ideas coherently and with organization, using appropriate vocabulary, grammar, and mechanics than they would when administering the more commonly utilized on-demand writing assessments.

The example assessment below is appropriate for upper elementary and middle school students. Ideally, it would be administered over a two-day block during one class period each day. A rubric for scoring the writing done on the second day is given on after the assessment.

Once the teacher has become familiarized with the general design of a Read-Write Cycle assessment, he or she is encouraged to create their own versions to assess writing across the curriculum.

Sample Read-Write Cycle Assessment—"Winning the Lottery

Day 1 of 2

Topic:	What would happen if my family (or I) won the Lottery?
Group Organization:	Whole class or partners
Teacher Materials:	Chart Paper, markers
Student Materials:	Text, Group task sheets
Time:	One class session, two days in a row

Note: Adjust the dialogue as appropriate for you and your students.

Pre-Reading: Introduce the activity. This segment should take 5-7 minutes.

<u>Connect</u>: **"What would happen if your family (or you) won the lottery?"**

[Option: individual quick write, partner brainstorm]

<u>Brainstorm</u>: **"Let's get some of your ideas on the chart paper. What would happen if your family (or you) won the lottery?"**

Prompts: **"What are some positive things?"**
"You've mentioned positives to having money. Any negatives?"

Prompt students with questions regarding:
- behaviors
- emotions
- relationships
- other

Vocabulary to highlight: millionaire, purchase, opinion

[Check and adjust text to meet your students' needs.]

<u>Organize</u>: **"Look at our brainstorming list. How might we group some of these ideas together? Let's think of some headings we could use to categorize the items we have on the list. We are going to organize the list by making a web. The web will help us think about our ideas. Now tell me where each item should go and why you think that is the best place for it."**

[Make a web with 'Winning the Lottery' in the center circle. Draw lines to circles surrounding the center circle, placing category titles in the surrounding circles. Place lines radiating out from the category title circles and write the appropriate items from the brainstorm list at the ends of the lines. Be sure to have the student justify the placement.]

[Students can make their own webs modeled on the class web.]

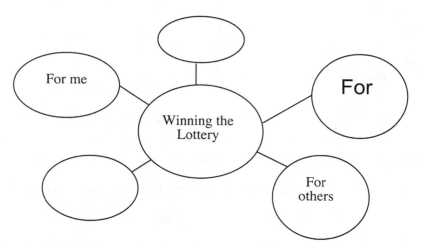

Purpose: **"During the next two days you will be talking and reading about what happens to people when they win large amounts of money – positive things and perhaps negative things. You will share your ideas and hear the ideas of others. Tomorrow you will write about how life would be different if you won the lottery. I will be looking at your writing to see the ways that you share your ideas on paper and to find what you like to write about. Later in the year, we will look at this piece of writing to see how you've developed as writers."**

Connect: [Lead into the text….]

Reading: Distribute the text. Students can read independently or with a partner.
[Note any additional support provided, i.e., teacher reading to a specific student.]
"As you read, think about the two questions on the side. Write down some notes either while you are reading or when you are finished." Plan about 5-7 minutes for reading and 5-7 minutes for individual responses to the passage.

Facilitate by drawing attention to the question and providing support/clarification as appropriate. [Since students read at various paces, have a plan for what they will do when finished.]

[Option: Whole-group discussion of student responses to questions.]

Post-Reading: Help students get started by introducing the activity as a whole-class discussion. Recreate the Venn diagram [see Group Task] on chart paper or overhead transparency. Explain the meaning of each section of the diagram [characteristics of having much money, little money, and commonalities.]

Organize: **"What is life like when you have lots of money?"**
*Once students begin generating ideas, move into smaller groups [see below].
Discussion prompts: **Tell us more about that.**
            Make connections between the sections.

Divide students into groups of 2 or 4. Have them continue comparing and contrasting life with and without money. [Use your judgment for effective arrangements based on your students' experiences with cooperative groups.]

Small Group Report: The purposes are (a) to add further ideas and vocabulary to the original webbing chart, and (b) focus individual students on the theme or position for the upcoming writing assignment.

"I'd like each group to share their Venn diagram. Tell us two or three of your items and where you put your items. If you hear something that you didn't think about for your Venn diagram, you can add it to yours."

Each group will have 1-2 minutes to share highlights from their Venn diagrams.

Closure: Re-cap by adding new information to the web [as appropriate].
"Tomorrow you will take this information, as well as the ideas you've heard from your classmates, and write about what your life would be like if you and your family won the lottery."

The dress is the lightest shade of blue: floor-length, fitted on top and flowing into a full skirt. It costs $139. For 15-year-old Cheyanne Maples, owning this dress would have been impossible in the past.

Today Cheyanne and her brother, John, don't even look at price tags as they shop for the big dance.

Three months ago, their mother, who worked at a company for 25 years, lost her job because the plant was shut down.

But the family got lucky! Just after losing the job, they became millionaires by winning the Lotto. The prize was beyond their wildest dreams! For the next 20 years, their mother will receive $135,000.

Shop till you drop

That money has meant changes for the family. The Maples purchased a satellite dish, a new dishwasher, and two new cars (one a Miata). They are planning to build a new house. Everyone is wearing new clothes.

The family agrees that shopping is the best part of winning the lottery.

Talk of the halls

At West Lake High School, where Cheyanne and John go to school, news of the big win spread fast. Everybody knew about their good luck – and everyone had an opinion about it.

On the first day, Cheyanne received a marriage proposal in the cafeteria ("He was on his knees right in front of my lunch tray!" she groans.)

Soon life got back to normal. Cheyanne still spends one class period working in the school office; John still stays after school to play chess.

It looks the same from the outside, but some things have changed. Cheyanne's friend Annie thinks the money's made Cheyanne forget her real friends. "I'm glad it wasn't me," she says, "money makes people do stupid things."

And Jason says, "John got a big head. All he talks about is what he's bought and what he's going to by next."

Cheyanne thinks people notice her more now. She asks, "Why didn't they like me before? It's not like I have any more money. My Mom does."

They also know that while money can change what you have, it cannot change who you are or what your parents expect from you. In the end, it's their money.

John might be able to buy expensive clothes, but he still gets in trouble for not putting his clothes in the dryer.

The bottom line?

Money can bring you wonderful things, but you'll still be the same person you always were, coping with the same stuff you always did.

What do you think about how the family decided to spend their money?

They got their money three months ago. What so you think their lives will be like in a year.

66

Sample Read-Write Cycle Assessment— "Winning the Lottery

Day 2 of 2

Topic: What would happen if I won the Lottery?
Group Organization: Whole class & individuals
Teacher Materials: Chart Paper, markers
Student Materials: Pre-writing worksheet, writing paper, previous day's materials
Time: One class session, two days in a row

Note: Adjust the dialogue as appropriate for you and your students.

Pre-Writing: Whole-class activity. Review the previous day's session, remind students of topic, webbing chart, and Venn diagram. Hand out the Pre-Writing Worksheet and instruct students about how to transfer key words from the webbing chart, and how to add their own words to the worksheet. You may also direct the students to include a graphic organizer [e.g., matrix, re-organized web, Venn diagram] as part of their planning. This segment should take about 5-6 minutes.

Writing: Individual task. The students will have access to the Pre-Writing Worksheet and the Webbing Chart (Day 1), and other resources allowed by the teacher, including dictionary and thesaurus. Remember, the goal is to obtain optimal performance. Students may ask the teacher for clarification about the task, but students may not help one another. This segment should take 12-15 minutes.

Post-Writing: Whole-class activity. Debrief class after the papers are turned in. **"How did you feel about the writing task?"** [words of advice, problems]. Students can briefly assess their performance [think to self, talk with a neighbor, provide an appropriate signal]. This segment should take 2-5 minutes.

Group Task: Venn Diagram

Name _____

Name _____

List 5 – 7 items in each section.

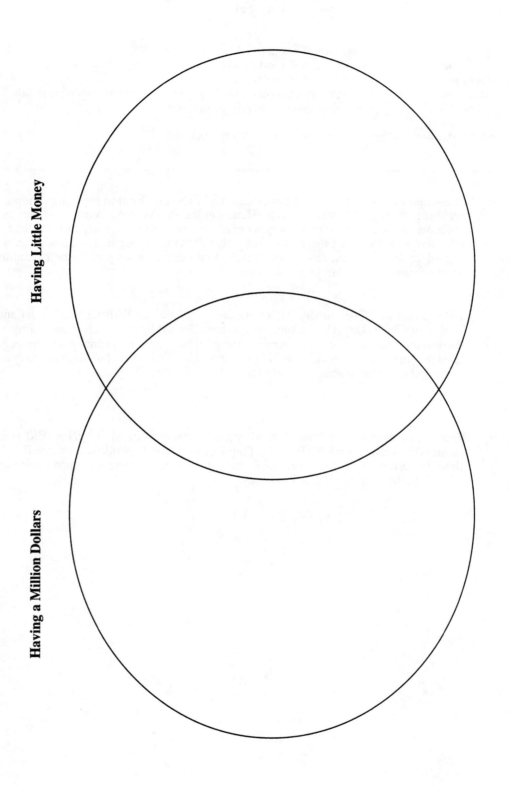

Having a Million Dollars

Having Little Money

Name _____   Date _____

_____

List 5 – 7 items for each question. Find words from the web and the Venn diagram that will help you when you write.
Use words, phrases, pictures, or sentences.

What would I do for <u>myself</u>?	What would my family do for <u>each other</u>?	What would my family and I do for <u>others</u>? [friends, neighbors, our community, strangers, etc.]

Winning the Lottery   Name _____ Date _____

Choose one topic. Write 1 – 2 pages about you and your family winning the lottery. Use your Pre-Writing Worksheet to get ideas and words for your paper. You can also use new ideas.

When you finish, read your paper again.

- Will the reader understand what you are thinking?
- Check for spelling. and grammar (periods, capitals, etc.)

1.   **If my family and I won the lottery,...**

or

2.   **I think that my family and I should win the lottery because...**

_____

_____

_____

_____

_____

_____

_____

_____

_____

_____

_____

_____

_____

_____

_____

_____

_____

_____

_____

_____

Read-Write Cycle Assessment Rubric

Score	Length	Coherence	Vocabulary	Grammar / Mechanics / Spelling
6	3 - 5 pages or 176 or more words	Clearly elaborated main topic. Support with appropriate details, descriptions and examples. Clear shifts in topic and smooth transitions.	Substantial use of complex Romance words. Lexical variety and precision in dealing with topic.	Few errors in grammar, punctuation, or spelling. Variety in sentence structures. Correct spelling of complex words.
5	1-2 pages or 86-175 words	Main topic is clearly stated and unwavering. Some support for selected points. Linkages are provided, but transitions are not always clear.	Some evidence of complex but familiar Romance words. Limited variety and reliance on relatively common words (national).	Some variation in sentence structure, including phrases and clauses. Command of long /short vowels, but other vowel errors (e.g., vowel digraphs).
4	3/4 page or 61-85 words	Topic is clear with digressions. Information and examples are plentiful but list-like.	Substantial number of familiar polysyllabic words (interesting, understand). Noticeable precision ('friendly' for 'nice').	Sentence completeness and variety, with few run-ons and fragments. Few errors in punctuation. Short vowels accurate, with emergence of long-short contrast.
3	4 sentences -- _ page or 36-60 words	Addresses the topic, but with little description, elaboration, or support.	1 - 2 syllable words, but mostly frequent and little variety or precision.	Simple repetitive sentences, fragments and run-ons. Consonants generally correct, with vowel omissions and substitutions, but readable.
2	2 - 3 sentences or 11-35 words	States the topic minimally, and wander off topic. Little support. .	Frequent one-syllable and basic sight words.	Many fragments / run-ons. Consonants generally correct, but omission of most vowels.
1	1 sentence or less or 0-10 words	Unrelated or unintelligible.	Most words difficult to interpret.	Generally unintelligible.

Report Notes

This form is to help the reader analyze the features of a report or exposition. It can also be used to plan for the writing of a research paper or summarizing a chapter.

MAIN TOPIC: Look over the title and skim the report headings and paragraphs. What is the article mostly about?

_____

_____

TYPE OF REPORT: Reports give information, explain a process, or argue a position. What is the purpose of this article?

_____

_____

INTRODUCTION/OVERVIEW: Read the first paragraph carefully. It should tell you what the article is going to do and why. If the first paragraph is really an introduction, write down the main points in this paragraph. Otherwise, tell what the paragraph does do.

_____

_____

SUMMARY: Sometimes the last paragraph goes through the main points. Skip to the end, read the last paragraph, and describe what you find there.

_____

_____

MAIN "CHUNKS:" Using what you have already written above, divide the article into no more than five "chunks," and summarize what happens in each of these in a sentence or two. Circle the KEY WORDS in each chunk.

#1_____

_____

#2_____

_____

#3_____

_____

#4_____

_____

#5_____

_____

SUMMARY: Now write your own summary of the article!

Story Notes

This form is to help the reader analyze the features of a story or narrative. It can also be used to plan for the writing of a book report or story.

SETTING: Where and when does the story take place? What do things look like, sound like, feel like?

_____

_____

THE BIG PROBLEM: In most stories, something is wrong that the characters need to fix. The problem sometimes isn't at the beginning, but turns up in the middle, or even at the end. What's the big problem?

_____

_____

CHARACTERS: Who are the most important characters, and what are they like – looks, personality, and so on. Write the name and then the characteristics.

_____ _____

_____ _____

_____ _____

_____ _____

PLOT: Describe the most important events in the story in a few words. Write the page number down so you can go back if you need to. Also write one or two key vocabulary words about the event.

#1_____

_____

#2_____

_____

#3_____

_____

#4_____

_____

#5_____

_____

RESOLUTION: How does the story end? How is the big problem settled or resolved?

_____

_____

Introduction to the Lesson Plans

The lesson plans we have included here all follow the Scaffolded Reading Experience model. The Scaffolded Reading Experience (SRE) is one of the frameworks for scaffolding students' reading described in Chapter 6 of *Teaching Reading in the 21st Century.* It is a framework that one of us has worked on for over 25 years and that is the topic of two books: *Scaffolding Reading Experiences: Designs for Student Success* (Graves & Graves, 1994, 2003) and *Scaffolding Reading Experiences for English-Language Learners* (Fitzgerald & Graves, in press). It is also the framework used in the *OnLine Reading Resources* Web site (www.onlinereadingresources.com), which contains detailed lesson plans for a number of widely used texts. It has been validated in research studies (Appleman & Liang, 2003; Cooke, 2002; Fournier & Graves, 2002, Graves & Liang, 2002; Watts & Rothenberg (1997). It is a very powerful and widely applicable framework. Both preservice and inservice teachers have told us that it is one of the most valuable and practical tools they have found for creating lessons that assist all students in reading, understanding, learning from, and enjoying each and every text they read. Teachers have also told us that the SRE framework is equally effective with students who struggle with reading, gifted readers, English-language learners, and native-English speakers.

As noted in Chapter 6, in the two SRE books, and on the Web site, the central concept underlying the approach is that of scaffolding. A scaffold is a temporary supportive structure that enables a reader to successfully complete a task she or he would not be able to complete without the aid of the scaffold. Additionally, scaffolding can aid students by helping them better complete a reading task, complete a reading task with less stress or in less time, or learn more fully than they would have without the aid of the scaffold.

The framework has two parts—the Planning Phase and the Implementation Phase—which are showing in the following figure. As shown in the upper half of the figure, the Planning Phase takes into account the students who are doing the reading, the text they are reading, and the purposes for reading it. Because different

The SRE Framework

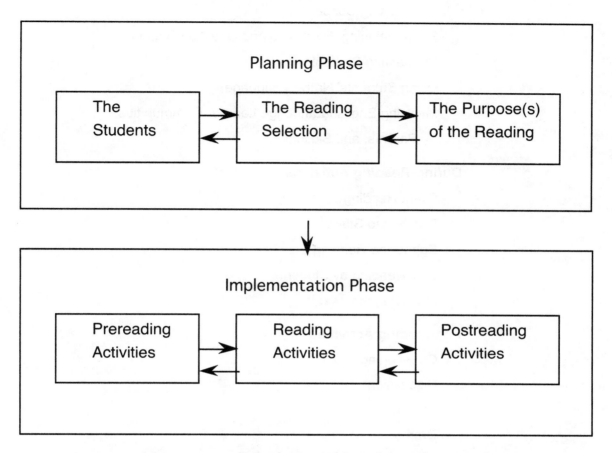

Taken with permission from Michael F. Graves & Bonnie B. Graves. (2003). *Scaffolding Reading Experiences: Designs for Student Success* (2nd ed.). Christopher-Gordon: Norwood, MA.

combinations of students, texts, and purposes call for very different activities, SREs take a variety of forms and no two are exactly alike. As shown in the lower half of the figure, the components of the Implementation Phase are prereading activities, during-reading activities, and postreading activities.

Here is a list of possible components of an SRE, including several components specifically designed to scaffold English-language learners' reading.

Prereading Activities

Motivating

Relating the Reading to Students' Lives

Activating Background Knowledge

Building Text-Specific Knowledge

Preteaching Vocabulary

Preteaching Concepts

Prequestioning, Predicting and Direction Setting

Suggesting Strategies

Using Students' Native Language

Involving English-Language Learner Communities,
Parents, and Siblings.

During-Reading Activities

Silent Reading

Reading to Students

Supported Reading

Oral Reading by Students

Modifying the Text

Postreading Activities

Questioning

Discussion

Writing

Drama

Artistic and Nonverbal Activities

Application and Outreach Activities

Building Connections

Reteaching

As can be seen, this list includes ten types of prereading activities, five types of during-reading activities, and eight types of postreading activities. It is important to note that this is a list of *possible* components of an SRE. No single SRE includes all of these activities. Each SRE includes a different combination of activities—a combination that is appropriate for the students, selection, and purpose for which the SRE is designed. For example, for one text and purpose, you might employ three prereading activities, and for another text and purpose you might use a single prereading activity.

Each type of SRE activity serves a different purpose: Prereading activities prepare students to read the upcoming selection. They can serve a number of functions in helping students engage with and comprehend text. These include piquing students' interest in the selection, reminding them of things they already know relevant to the selection, and preteaching aspects of the selection that they may find difficult, such as complex concepts and troublesome words. Of course, students can read many texts without prereading assistance; but when texts are challenging or when you want students to understand them deeply and want to assist them in becoming better readers and thinkers, prereading activities can set the stage for a truly productive and rewarding reading experience.

During-Reading activities support and guide students as they are reading. During-reading activities include both things that students do themselves as they are reading and things that you do to assist them as they are reading—students reading silently, your reading to them, students taking notes as they read, and the like.

Postreading activities provide opportunities for students to synthesize and organize information gleaned from the text so that they can understand and recall important points and build their thinking and reasoning skills. Postreading activities also provide opportunities for students to evaluate an author's message, his or her stance in presenting the message, and the quality of the text itself. And they provide opportunities for students to respond to a text in a variety of ways—to reflect on the meaning of the text, to compare differing texts and ideas, to engage in a variety of activities that will refine and extend their understanding of what they learn from the text, to increase their higher order thinking skills, and to apply what they have learned to the world beyond the classroom.

The SRE framework is appropriate for virtually any combination of texts and purposes; but the specific pre-, during-, and postreading activities employed in any particular situation will differ greatly. In general, with more difficult selections and more challenging purposes, more scaffolding is needed. Conversely, with less difficult selections and less challenging purposes, less scaffolding is needed. The scaffolded reading framework is flexible and adaptable in that it presents a variety of options—sets of pre-, during-, and postreading options—from which you choose as you create a lesson.

Included in the remainder of this booklet are complete and detailed Scaffolded Reading Experiences for three reading selections. The first *And the DISH Ran Away with the SPOON* is appropriate for the primary grades, the second *Because of Winn-Dixie* is appropriate for the upper elementary grades, and the third *Black Powder,* is appropriate for the middle grades.

Since each individual SRE is designed for a specific text, each of them contains different teaching and learning activities. However, in order to facilitate your use of the individual SREs on this Web site, each SRE contains the same eight sections. These are listed and briefly described below:

(1) Table of Contents. This lists the following seven sections of the SRE and provides a hyperlink to each of them.

(2) Introduction. This is a brief introduction to the text and, in some cases, the author.

(3) Objectives. Here, we list the major objectives for the SRE.

(4) Higher Order Thinking Skills. Here, we list the higher order thinking skills emphasized in the SRE.

(5) Chronological List of Activities. This section provides a list of activities for the SRE in an outline form. Activities include a selection of the pre-reading, during-reading, and post-reading alternatives listed above.

(6) Detailed Description of Activities. This section describes the activities for the SRE in detail.

(7) Student Materials. This section provides the actual materials used in teaching a reading selection, for example, previews, discussion questions, and writing activities.

(8) Sources of the Reading Selection, Additional Readings, and Other Material. This section includes a source or sources of the reading selection itself, including an Internet source if there is one, and supplementary materials to facilitate your teaching it. Possible supplementary materials include criticism or book reviews, multimedia materials, additional readings by the same author, additional readings on the same topic, Internet sites, and references.

You can use the lessons plans as they are with your students, you can modify them so that they particularly fit your style of teaching and your specific students, and you can use them as models of carefully planned and effective lesson plans that will assist you in planning your own lessons.

References

Appleman, D. A., & Liang, L. A. (2003). *Scaffolding students' reading experiences: A framework for diverse learners.* Paper submitted for publication at the 2003 meeting of the National Reading Conference.

Cooke, C. L. (2002). *The effects of scaffolding multicultural short stories on students' comprehension, response, and attitudes.* Unpublished doctoral dissertation, University of Minnesota, Minneapolis.

Fitzgerald, J. & Graves, M. F. (in press). *Scaffolding reading experiences for English-language learners.* Norwood, MA: Christopher-Gordon.

Fournier, D. N. E., & Graves, M. F. (2002). Scaffolding adolescents' comprehension of short stories. *Journal of Adolescent and Adult Literacy, 40,* 30-39.

Graves, M. F., & Graves, B. B. (1994, 2003). *Scaffolding reading experiences: Designs for student success* (1st and 2nd eds.). Norwood, MA: Christopher-Gordon.

Graves, M. F., & Liang, L. A. (2003). On-line resources for fostering understanding and higher-level thinking in senior high school students. Schallert, D. L., Fairbanks, C. M., Worthy, J. Maloch, B., & Hoffman, J. V. (Eds.), *51st Yearbook of the National Reading Conference Yearbook* (pp. 204-215). Oak Creek, WI: National Reading Conference.

Watts S. M., & Rothenberg, S. S. (1997). Students with learning difficulties meet Shakespeare: Using a scaffolded reading experience. *Journal of Adolescent & Adult Literacy, 40,* 532-539.

Scaffolded Reading Experience™ for Fostering Higher Order Reading and Comprehension Skills

with

And the DISH Ran Away with the SPOON

by Janet Stevens and Susan Stevens Crummel

An SRE™ created by Cheryl Peterson
University of Minnesota
© 2003 Seward Learning Systems, Inc.
Available at OnLine Reading Resources
onlinereadingresources.com

Table of Contents

Introduction

Hey Diddle Diddle, the cat and the fiddle, The cow jumped over the moon; The little dog laughed to see such sport, And the dish ran away with the spoon.

— *From* And the Dish Ran Away with the Spoon

With the end of this familiar nursery rhyme, the adventure is just beginning. Janet Stevens and Susan Stevens Crummel spin a wonderful tale through fairy tale land telling the story of what happens after Dish and Spoon run away. The reader is led by the cat, the dog, and the cow with a map of fairy tale land to track down the missing dish and spoon. Filled with idioms and illustrations with clues and hints about various fairy tale and nursery rhyme characters, this book will delight children and adults.

The picture book is written at a primary grade level, and is also an excellent choice for a read-aloud. This Scaffolded Reading Experience (SRE) is geared to first through third grades and could be easily adapted for kindergarten. The SRE is designed to encourage students' thorough enjoyment of the picture book, and to appreciate how the sequence of the story helps to build the plot. The SRE also uses strategies well-suited for primary grade students, such as partner and group work, listening skills, and practice at reading skills such as making predictions.

Objectives

- To foster students' enjoyment of a creative text.

- To give students experience making plausible predictions and inferences about a fiction text.

- To help students recognize and understand idioms.

- To help develop students' ability to see how maps can be useful tools for decision making.

Higher Order Thinking Skills

- Understanding—Constructing meaning from instructional messages, including oral, written, and graphic communications.

- Analyzing—Breaking material into its constituent parts and determining how the parts relate to one another and to an overall structure or purpose.

- Creating—Putting elements together to form a coherent or functional whole, reorganizing elements into a new pattern or structure.

Chronological List of Activities

Day 1

Pre-Reading Activity

(1) Motivating Activity, *5 minutes*

During-Reading Activity

(1) Guided Reading, *15 minutes*

Post-Reading Activity

(1) Artistic Activity, *15 minutes*

Day 2

Pre-Reading Activities

(1) Predicting, 10 minutes

(2) Direction Setting, *5 minutes*

During-Reading Activity

(1) Reading Aloud to Students, *10 minutes*

Post-Reading Activity

(1) Class Discussion, *10 minutes*

Day 3

Post-Reading Activity

(1) Graphic Activity, *35 minutes*

Day 4

Pre-Reading Activities

(1) Preteaching Concepts, *5 minutes*

(2) Direction Setting, *5 minutes*

During-Reading Activity

(1) Reading Aloud to Students, *10 minutes*

Post-Reading Activities

(1) Discussion, 5 minutes

(2) Artistic Activity, *10 minutes*

Day 5

Post-Reading Activity

(1) Writing Activity, *35 minutes*

Detailed Description of Activities

Day 1

Pre-Reading Activity

1. *Motivating Activity, 5 minutes*

- Tell students that tomorrow they will be reading a story that has a lot of different nursery rhyme and fairy tale stories in it. In order to enjoy the story, they are going to read some nursery rhymes and fairy tales

During-Reading Activity

1. *Guided Reading, 15 minutes*

- Assign groups of 2-3 students one of the fairy tales or nursery rhymes from *And the Dish Ran Away with the Spoon*.

- Instruct student groups to read the fairy tale or nursery rhyme and pay attention to details about the characters and the setting.

- See the Student Materials for a list of the nursery rhymes and fairy tales to use.

Post-Reading Activity

1. *Artistic Activity, 15 minutes*

- Give student groups a sheet of construction paper.

- Instruct students to draw the characters and setting fairy tale or nursery rhyme that they read in as much detail as possible.

Day 2

Pre-Reading Activities

1. *Predicting, 10 minutes*

- Read aloud to students the first page of the book *And the DISH Ran Away with the SPOON* by Jane Stevens and Susan Crummel, which introduces the traditional nursery rhyme.

- Close the book and show students the cover and read the title. Ask students to predict what this story might be about.

- Then, ask students what they think might happen to the dish and the spoon.

- Record students' ideas on a chart, chalkboard or sentence strips.

2. Direction Setting, 5 minutes

- Hand out to students groups their pictures from the previous day.

- Ask students to listen for clues about the fairy tale or nursery rhyme that they illustrated while you are reading.

- Instruct students to quietly hold up their picture when they hear or see a clue from their fairy tale or nursery rhyme.

During-Reading Activity

1. Reading Aloud to Students, 10 minutes

- Read the book *And the Dish Ran Away with the Spoon* aloud to students.

- While reading, give students time to view the pictures and catch the various references to other fairy tales and nursery rhymes.

- Remind students if necessary to hold up the appropriate illustration when they hear their fairy tale mentioned.

Post-Reading Activity

1. Class Discussion, 10 minutes

- After the chart from the previous activity is finished, tell students that in a moment you will start reading Chapter 5. But, first, ask if any students have predictions regarding what Nick's report will be like, and discuss their predictions.

- Discuss with students the ways the various fairy tales and nursery rhymes were woven throughout the story.

- Refer back to the text to check details and reinforce this point.

Day 3

Post-Reading Activity

1. *Graphic activity, 35 minutes*

   - Use a bulletin board or large sheet of butcher paper to construct a map of fairy tale land based on the information presented in the book.

   - Start by placing a picture of the dog, cat, and cow in the lower, middle part of the map. Ask students if they remember where the animals traveled first. Refer back to the book if necessary (p.10).

   - Then place a fork just north of the starting point. Refer to the text directions, "the Three Bears live on mile east and Little Boy Blue's haystack is one mile west." (p.13). Discuss with students where to place the illustrations they constructed on Day 1 on the map.

   - Continue following the directions in the book until all of the illustrations have been added to the map.

   - Add any appropriate details or mapping symbols.

Day 4

Pre-Reading Activities

1. *Preteaching Concepts, 5 minutes*

   - Explain to students that idioms are groups of words that really don't mean what they say. They are confusing because they have a special meaning and if you don't know the meaning you won't understand what they mean.

   - Share with students the example of "a fork in the road," (p.10). Ask students what these words make them picture. Show the picture on page 10 of a fork in the road. Ask students what they think this saying really means. Share with students that a fork in the road is a place in a road where they can go different directions.

   - Share with students the examples of idioms from the student activity page and discuss what the words make them think and their meaning. Explain why these are examples of idioms.

2. Direction Setting, 5 minutes

- Tell students that today you are going to again read <u>And the Dish Ran Away with the Spoon</u>, but instead of watching for fairy tales and nursery rhymes you want them to point out idioms.

- Tell them that when they hear an idiom to raise their hand and you will write it on a sentence strip.

During-Reading Activity

1. Reading Aloud to Students, 10 minutes

- Read the story aloud to students.

- As students point out the idioms, write them or have a student write them on a sentence strip.

- Then ask students what the idiom means. If students point out sayings that are not idioms, discuss why they are not idioms.

- Point out or help students find the idioms that they do not discover on their own. The idioms and their meanings are listed in the student activity pages.

Post-Reading Activities

1. Discussion, 5 minutes

- Take each of the idioms the students found and discuss the meaning found in the story versus the real meaning.

2. Artistic Activity, 10 minutes

- Give students a sheet of construction paper and one of the sentence strips with an idiom written on it.

- Instruct students to fold the construction paper in half.

- On the left side students should draw the meaning that they think of when they just read the words.

- On the right side, students should draw an example of the meaning of the idiom.

- Instruct students to print the idiom on the back by copying the sentence strip.

- The sentence strips and pictures can then be used as an interactive bulletin board or the pictures can be used as a center activity. Students can try to guess the idiom represented by the pictures and then look on the back to check.

Day 5

Post-Reading Activity

1. Writing activity, 35 minutes

- This writing activity provides students with an opportunity to create and write their own variant tale.

- Show students the list of possible endings that they came up with for the story on Day 2.

- Tell students that their ideas could make interesting stories also.

- Instruct students to select one of the endings and write a story to go with it. Students may also be encouraged to use idioms in their writing.

- Have students share their stories with each other or compile them in a class book.

Student Materials

Student materials for *And the DISH Ran Away with the SPOON* includes a list of fairy tales and nursery rhymes, and a list of idioms and their meanings

- List of Fairy Tales and Nursery Rhymes for *And the DISH Ran Away with the SPOON*. This is list of the 12 fairy tales and nursery rhymes with corresponding page numbers as referenced in *And the DISH Ran Away with the SPOON*.

- List of Idioms and Their Meanings for *And the DISH Ran Away with the SPOON*. This is a list of 18 idioms found in *And the Dish Ran Away with the Spoon* and their meanings.

List of Fairy Tales and Nursery Rhymes for _And the DISH Ran Away with the SPOON_

- Four-and-twenty Blackbirds, p.10

- House that Jack Built, p.12, 38, 39

- Humpty Dumpty, p.12, 38, 41

- Jack and the Beanstalk, p.12, 30, 36

- Jack Be Nimble, p. 39

- Little Bo Peep, p.10, 12

- Little Boy Blue, p.12, 13,15,17

- Little Miss Muffet, p.12, 17, 19

- Rub – a – Dub Dub, p.12, 26

- The Three Bears, p.13

- The Three Little Pigs, p. 21, 26

- Three Blind Mice, p. 40, 42

List of Idioms and Their Meanings for *And the DISH Ran Away with the SPOON*

Idiom	Meaning
dog-tired	Very tired
fork in the road	A point in the road where you can go different directions
in a jam	In a bad situation
take a stab at it	Try it
hit the hay	Go to bed
hey fever	Allergies to hay
in a pickle	In a bad situation
nothing to sneeze at	A big problem
barking up the wrong tree	Trying the wrong thing
neck of the woods	A particular area
don't be a chicken	Don't be afraid
his bark is worse than his bite	He sounds meaner than he really is
a close shave	Something almost happened but didn't
not out of the woods yet	Not safe yet
there in a flash	There soon
went to pieces	Really upset
stuck with it	Kept working on something
when the chips are down	When things look hopeless

Sources of the Reading Selection, Additional Readings, and Other Material

Source of the Reading Selection

Stevens, J. and Stevens Crummel, S. (2001). And the DISH Ran Away with the SPOON. San Diego: Harcourt, Inc.

Criticism / Book Reviews

Sims, Michael (2001). And the Dish Ran Away with the Spoon Review. Children's BookPage. c

Other Nursery Rhyme and Fairy Tale Books

Adams, P. ill. (1995). *This Is the House That Jack Built.* New York: Childs Play Intl. Ltd.

Beaton, C. (2000). *Mother Goose Remembers.* New York: Barefoot Books.

Brett, J. (1996). *Goldilocks and the Three Bears.* New York: Paper Star.

Galdone, P. (1984). *The Three Little Pigs.* New York: Houghton Mifflin.

Gliori, D. ill. (2001). *The Dorling Kindersley Book of Nursery Rhymes.* New York: DK Publishing.

Gorbachev, V. (2001). *Goldilocks and the Three Bears.* New York: North South Books.

Grover, E. ed. (1997). *Mother Goose: The Original Volland Edition.* New York: Outlet.

Kellogg, S. (1997). *Jack and the Beanstalk.* New York: Mulberry Books.

Montgomery, W. ed. (2002). *Over the Candlestick: Classic Nursery Rhymes and the Real Stories Behind Them.* New York: Peachtree Pub. Ltd.

Other Variant Tales (Variant tales are stories that are based on traditional stories but add alternative details or endings.)

Aylesworth, Jim. (1990). *The Completed Hickory Dickory Dock.* New York: Aladdin Books.

Miranda, A. (1997). *To Market, to Market.* New York: Harcourt, Inc.

Scieszka, J. (1989). *The True Story of the 3 Little Pigs.* New York: Scholastic.

Idioms

Gwynne, F. (1988). *The King Who Rained.* New York: Aladdin Books.

Terban, M. (1983). *In a Pickle: And Other Funny Idioms.* New York: Houghton Mifflin Co.

Terban, M. (1993). *It Figures! Fun Figures of Speech.* New York: Clarion Books.

Terban, M. (1987). *Mad as a Wet Hen: And Other Funny Idioms.* New York: Houghton Mifflin Co.

Terban, M. (1990). *Punching the Clock: Funny Action Idioms.* New York: Clarion Books.

Internet Sites

http://childhoodreading.com/ - This site contains a collection of illustrated fables, folk, and fairy tales.

http://mamalisa.com/house - This site contains colorfully illustrated Mother Goose rhymes.

www.goosie.com/kids/ - This site contains fairy tales with a modern twist and coordinating recipes.

http://www.zelo.com/family/nursery/ - This site contains an extensive collection of nursery rhymes.

Scaffolded Reading Experience™ for Fostering Higher Order Reading and Comprehension Skills

with

Because of Winn-Dixie

by Kate DiCamillo

Created by Lauren A. Liang
University of Minnesota,

Table of Contents

Introduction

> "Take one disarmingly engaging protagonist and put her in the company of a tenderly rendered canine, and you've got yourself a recipe for the best kind of down-home literary treat. Kate DiCamillo's voice in *Because of Winn-Dixie* should carry from the steamy, sultry pockets of Florida clear across the miles to enchant young readers everywhere."
>
> *-Karen Hesse*

With the support of the 1998 McKnight Artist Fellowship for Writers and a local writing group, author Kate DiCamillo wove an engaging story for children starring thoughtful, 10-year old India Opal and her beloved friend and pet dog, Winn-Dixie. The resulting book, *Because of Winn-Dixie*, has received much praise, including being named as a 2001 Newbery Honor book and a 2001 Riverbank Review Children's Book of Distinction.

The well-developed characters, universal themes of friendships and grief, and the lyrical prose of the novel have helped make it very popular with children in the intermediate grades. The protagonist, Opal, is a lonely child and searches for friends in the new town to which she and her father have recently moved. The diversity of the friends she gradually makes—from an elderly librarian to a guitar-playing ex-felon who works in the local pet store—and the way she brings them together as a community make for an entertaining tale.

This Scaffolded Reading Experience focuses on these strengths of the novel, making use of DiCamillo's rich and memorable cast of characters. The SRE is designed to help students develop the skills of identifying character traits and distinguish between personal attributes and physical traits, and to see clearly how authors develop the personality of their characters. Students are asked to use textual quotes as "evidence" of certain traits of individual characters. The SRE was developed particularly for fifth and sixth graders, and uses strategies such as partner and group work and repeated trials at various tasks, and practice at reading skills such as making predictions.

Objectives

- To introduce students to two types of character traits: personal attributes and physical traits

- To give students experience using textual quotes to support an opinion or judgment

- To give students experience making predictions in fiction stories

- To help develop students' awareness of character development in novels

Higher-Order Thinking Skills

- Understanding — Constructing meaning from instructional messages, including oral, written, and graphic communications.

- Analyzing — Breaking material into its constituent parts and determining how the parts relate to one another and to an overall structure or purpose.

- Evaluating — Making judgments based on criteria and standards.

Chronological List of Activities

Day 1

Prereading Activity

1. Relating the Reading to Students' Lives *20 minutes*

During Reading Activity

1. Reading to Students *20- 25 minutes*

During Reading Activity (as homework)

1. Silent Reading *as homework*

Day 2

Postreading Activity

1. Questioning *5 minutes*

Prereading Activities

1. Preteaching Concepts *20 minutes*

2. Direction Setting *15 minutes*

During Reading Activity (as homework)

1. Silent Reading *as homework*

Postreading Activity (as homework)

1. Writing *as homework*

Day 3

Postreading Activity

1. Discussion *10 minutes*

Prereading Activity

1. Predicting *10 minutes*

During Reading Activity

1. Reading to Students *15 minutes*

Prereading Activity

1. Predicting *5 minutes*

During Reading Activity (as homework)

1. Silent Reading *as homework*

Postreading Activity (as homework)

1. Writing *as homework*

Day 4

Postreading Activity

1. Graphic Activity *45 minutes*

Prereading Activity

1. Building Background Knowledge *5 minutes*

During Reading Activity (as homework)

1. Silent Reading *as homework*

Postreading Activity (as homework)

1. Writing *as homework*

Day 5

Postreading Activity

1. Discussion 5 *minutes*

During Reading Activity

1. Reading to Students *15 minutes*

Post Reading Activity

1. Discussion *20 minutes*

During Reading Activity (as homework)

1. Silent Reading *as homework*

Postreading Activity (as homework)

1. Writing *as homework*

Day 6

   Postreading Activities

   1.   Drama and Writing *40 minutes*

   2.   Discussion *5 minutes*

   Prereading Activity

   1.   Predicting *5 minutes*

   During Reading Activity (as homework)

   1.   Silent Reading *as homework*

   Postreading Activity (as homework)

   1.   Writing *as homework*

Day 7

   Postreading Activity

   1.   Discussion *10 minutes*

   Prereading Activity

   1.   Predicting *5 minutes*

   During Reading Activity

   1.   Reading to Students *25 minutes*

   During Reading Activity (as homework)

   1.   Silent Reading *as homework*

   Postreading Activity (as homework)

   1.   Writing *as homework*

Day 8

   Postreading Activity

   1.   Discussion *10 minutes*

   During Reading Activity

   1.   Reading to Students *15 minutes*

Postreading Activities

1. Questioning *20 minutes*

Day 9-10 and as homework

Postreading Activities

1. Artistic and Graphic Activities and Writing *60-120 minutes*

2. Discussion *20- 30 minutes*

Optional Additional Activities

Postreading Activity

1. Artistic and Graphic Activities, Writing, and/or Drama

Detailed Description of Activities

Day 1

Prereading Activity

1. Relating the Reading to Student's Lives 20 minutes

Hand out the story preview to students and read it aloud together. (See Student Materials.) Then have students write for five minutes about a time they experienced moving or being the newcomer in a situation at camp, school, etc. After five minutes of writing, have students share their writing with a partner in a two minute pair-share (In a two-minute pair-share, each student has two minutes to talk without any interruptions about what they wrote. After each partner has had two minutes, allow two minutes for students to ask one another questions or offer comments.) Then ask students to share to the whole group if they so desire.

Next, brainstorm as a whole class ways to make new friends when you are new to a place. After generating a short list of possibilities, tell students the book they are about to read is about a 10 year old girl who moves to a new town in Florida, and the experiences she has as she gets used to her new surroundings and makes friends, as well as dealing with some of the past experiences she has had in her life.

During Reading Activity

1. Reading to Students 20-25 minutes

Have students open their books and follow along as you read aloud the first two chapters. Discuss the definition of "missionary" when you come across the word. You may also need to describe "Winn-Dixie" if students are unfamiliar with the store.

104

During Reading Activity (as homework)

1. Silent Reading

Have students read Chapters 3 and 4 for homework.

Day 2

Postreading Activity

1. Questioning 5 minutes

On the board or overhead, have students help write the list of 10 things Opal finds out about her mother.

Prereading Activities

1. Preteaching Concepts 20 minutes

Ask students which of the items are physical traits; that is, things that describe Mama's physical appearance. Label these items "P. T." Then have students look at the remaining items. Explain that these items describe Mama in a different way: They are all examples of personal attributes Mama has. Tell students that when we describe a person, we often use both physical traits and personal attributes. For example, Brian is tall with brown hair and very patient with younger children. Then ask students, "How does an author let the reader get to know a character?" Brainstorm ideas, ultimately leading students to see that authors, most of the time, develop characters through physical descriptions, dialogue with others, inner thoughts, and actions. Through these ways, we get a picture of that character and his or her personality. Tell students that while they read this book, they are going to be looking and talking about the "character traits" of the characters. They'll be finding quotes in the story that show physical traits and personal attributes each character has.

Have students practice this idea of using physical traits and personal attributes for description by choosing a person they know well (their mom or dad, brother or sister, or best friend) and making a list of 5 physical traits and 5 personal attributes of that person. Circle the room and check students' work to see if they have the right idea. Have students share some of the personal attributes they came up with. Then pass out the list of possible Personal Attributes (See Student Materials.) Explain that this is only a partial list and that they should add more ideas to the list.

Now ask student to think about the character of Opal. Based on what they have read so far, what personal attributes does Opal have? As students suggest ideas, ask them to explain why they think that attribute fits and back up their reason with a specific quote from the book. You will likely need to guide students to find quotes. For example, if a student suggests Opal is brave because she saved Winn-Dixie from the pound, have students look at page 9 and 10 and find the quote that supports this idea: "Wait a minute!" I hollered. "That's my dog. Don't call the pound." All the Winn-Dixie employees turned around and looked at me, and I knew I had done something big. And maybe stupid, too. But I couldn't help it. I couldn't let that dog go to the pound."

2. *Direction Setting 15 minutes*

Pass out the Double-Entry Journal guide (See Student Materials) to students. Read through the guide with students and explain they will be responsible for doing an entry for each chapter assigned for homework. They must do personal attributes and not physical traits, and should do two for each chapter (These do not have to be for the same character.) Demonstrate an example on the board or overhead using a personal attribute for Opal that was just suggested.

During Reading Activity (as homework)

1. Silent Reading

Have students read Chapters 5 and 6 for homework.

Postreading Activity

1. Writing

Students should write in their double entry journals for each chapter (Two personal attributes with textual evidence per chapter.)

Day 3

Postreading Activity

1. Discussion 10 minutes

Begin by having students briefly share their double-entry journal assignments, either with partners or in small groups. Ask a few students to volunteer examples to the whole class.

Then as a whole class, briefly discuss Opal's adaptation to her new town so far. Does it seem like she has made any new friends?

Prereading Activity

1. Predicting 10 minutes

Give students three or four minutes to write down their predictions of what Miss Fanny's story might be. Share a few of these ideas as a whole class

During Reading Activity

1. Reading to Students 15 minutes

Read aloud Chapter 7 to the students while they follow along.

Prereading Activity

1. Predicting 5 minutes

Have students make predictions about Amanda and the role she will play in the book.

During Reading Activity (as homework)

1. Silent Reading

Have students read Chapters 8, 9, and 10 for homework.

Postreading Activity (as homework)

1. Writing

Students should write in their double-entry journals for each chapter. (Two personal attributes with textual evidence for each chapter.)

Day 4

Postreading Activity

1. Graphic Activity 45 minutes

Have students in partner groups create a list of all the characters in the book so far. For each character, they should list two personal attributes next to the character's name. Next to these two traits, have the students draw the character, showing two physical traits in the picture.

Have students share their work with each other.

Prereading Activity

1. *Building Background Knowledge 5 minutes*

    Discuss briefly with students how animals often react to storms.

During Reading Activity (as homework)

1. *Silent Reading*

    Have students read Chapters 11, 12, and 13 for homework.

Postreading Activity (as homework)

1. *Writing*

    Students should write in their double-entry journals for each chapter. (Two

personal attributes with textual evidence for each chapter.)

Day 5

Postreading Activity

1. *Discussion 5 minutes*

    Ask students to share one of the personal attributes they discovered in last night's

reading, and the textual evidence they wrote down as the supportive quote.

During Reading Activity

1. *Reading to Students 15 minutes*

    Read aloud Chapter 14 to students as they follow along.

Postreading Activity

1. Discussion 20 minutes

Have students reread the lines on page 96 that say "Judge them by what they are doing now." Then ask students if they would rather be judged by what they are doing right now or by what they were like in the past. Have students debate this idea in small groups and then as a whole class.

During Reading Activity (as homework)

1. Silent Reading

Have students read Chapters 15, 16, and 17 for homework.

Postreading Activity (as homework)

1. Writing

Students should write in their double-entry journals for each chapter. (Two personal attributes with textual evidence for each chapter.)

Day 6

Postreading Activities

1. Writing and Drama 40 minutes

On the board or overhead, write the word "bittersweet." Give students 10 to 15 minutes to write about an experience in their lives that they would call "bittersweet." After the writing time is over, have students share their stories with small groups. Then have each small group of students choose one story to act out in a brief skit for the class. Allow a few of the groups to act out their stories for the class.

2. *Discussion 5 minutes*

As a whole class, briefly discuss why India Opal's life is "bittersweet."

Prereading Activity

1. *Predicting 5 minutes*

Have students predict what they think will happen next in the story.

During Reading Activity (as homework)

1. *Silent Reading*

Have students read Chapters 18, 19, and 20 for homework.

Postreading Activity (as homework)

1. *Writing*

Students should write in their double-entry journals for each chapter. (Two personal attributes with textual evidence for each chapter.)

Day 7

Postreading Activity

1. *Discussion 10 minutes*

Have students pull out their double-entry journal assignments. Looking at what they have written, does it look like any of the characters have changed and may show different personal attributes than they did before? Have students give examples from the text that show characters may have changed.

Prereading Activity

1. Predicting 5 minutes

Have students predict what will happen at the party.

During Reading Activity

1. Reading to Students 25 minutes

Read aloud chapters 21 and 22 to your students.

During Reading Activity (as homework)

1. Silent Reading

Have students read Chapters 23, 24, and 25 for homework.

Postreading Activity (as homework)

1. Writing

Students should write in their double-entry journals for each chapter. (Two personal attributes with textual evidence for each chapter.)

Day 8

Postreading Activity

1. Discussion 10 minutes

Have students share with partners their favorite parts of the last four chapters in the book. Share a few of these as a whole class.

During Reading Activity

1. Reading to Students 15 minutes

Read aloud Chapter 26 to students.

Postreading Activity

1. Questioning 20 minutes

Have students respond in writing to two questions:

     (1) Why is 10 things not enough?

     (2) Do you think the ending is positive or negative? Why?

If time allows, you may want to discuss these questions orally.

Days 9-10

Postreading Activities

1. Graphic and Artistic Activities and Writing 60 –120 minutes and as homework

As a final activity for the book, have students work on the following assignment in class and as homework: "Make a poster featuring one of the characters in the story. The poster must contain a picture of the character exhibiting three physical traits that were mentioned in the story. These traits should be labeled and a quote from the text written by the label as "evidence." Underneath the picture, list five personal attributes of the character with a quote from the text to support each attribute. At the very bottom of the poster, write what is "bittersweet" for that character." (See Student Materials.)

2. Discussion 20-30 minutes

Allow students to view one another's posters and make positive comments. One way you can do this is to have students place their posters on their desks and rotate seats every few minutes. A piece of paper left at the desk can be used for the "visiting" students to write a positive comment.

Optional Additional Activities

1. Write an essay about an experience you have had that is bittersweet. [Note: This essay can be used as part of the Personal Narrative Minnesota Graduation Standard for the Intermediate Level (Write and Speak.)]

2. Read Kate DiCamillo's newest book, *The Tiger Rising* (Candlewick Press, 2001.) How is it bittersweet? Compare India Opal to Rob of *The Tiger Rising*.

2. Draw a picture of one of the scenes in the book that you think is very important to revealing one of the character's personality traits. Explain in writing why you think this scene is important for that reason.

3. Write a song (lyrics only to a tune you know or the tune and the lyrics) that Oliver might sing to his pets in the store. Explain why you think Oliver would sing this song.

Student Materials

Student materials for *Because of Winn-Dixie* include a preview, a possible personal attributes (character traits)" handout, a *Because of Winn-Dixie* double-entry journal handout, and a *Because of Winn-Dixie* final project.

- Preview for *Because of Winn-Dixie.* A preview (Graves, Prenn, & Cooke, 1985) is a well-crafted introduction to a text that is read to students prior to their reading the text itself. Previews include an introduction designed to gain students' attention, an overview of the text up to a suitable stopping place, and brief directions for reading.

- *Because of Winn-Dixie* Possible Personal Attributes (Character Traits) Handout. This handout lists attributes that characters might have.

- *Because of Winn-Dixie* Double-Entry Journal Handout. A form for listing character traits and quotes indicating those traits.

- *Because of Winn-Dixie* Final Project. Instructions for creating the final project, a poster with specific characteristics.

Preview for *Because of Winn-Dixie*

Have you ever moved to a new town? Or transferred to a new school with very few people you know? Or maybe gone to a summer camp away from home? Most people at one point or another have experienced what it is like to be new to a place. Perhaps the biggest challenge of being the newcomer is making friends. Think back to a time when you were the new person. How did it feel to not know anyone? Did you try to start conversations with others? Did you watch people closely? Can you remember what it felt like when you first met someone who might be a friend?

In *Because of Winn-Dixie*, you will meet India Opal, a ten-year-old girl who has just moved to a new town in Florida. You'll go along with her as she begins to get used to her new home and make friends.   You will hear her first impressions of the people she meets, and see if any of those impressions change. You may also see that moving to the new town could change Opal, too.

Because of Winn-Dixie Possible Personal Attributes (Character Traits) Handout

Agreeable	Enthusiastic	Kind	Self-sacrificing
Aggressive	Fearless	Lazy	Self-centered
Ambitious	Flexible	Loyal	Selfish
Angry	Foolish	Merciful	Sensible
Appreciative	Friendly	Mischievous	Serious
Arrogant	Generous	Modest	Servile
Bashful	Gentle	Narrow-minded	Shy
Boastful	Grouchy	Noble	Stubborn
Brave	Gullible	Obedient	Subservient
Calculating	Hard-working	Observant	Superstitious
Candid	Honest	Overconfident	Suspicious
Cautious	Honorable	Patient	Thoughtful
Clever	Humble	Perceptive	Thoughtless
Conceited	Humorous	Persistent	Timid
Confident	Imaginative	Proud	Trusting
Considerate	Impatient	Reasonable	Uncooperative
Cooperative	Impulsive	Reliable	Understanding
Courageous	Inconsiderate	Responsible	Unreasonable
Curious	Independent	Rigid	Unselfish
Deceitful	Industrious	Sarcastic	Wise
Determined	Insecure	Scornful	
Dishonest	Insincere	Self-conscious	

Because of Winn-Dixie Double-Entry Journal Assignment

For each chapter of Kate DiCamillo's *Because of Winn-Dixie* you will create a page in your character double-entry journal. Use the format below and the sample entry to help you.

Today's Date:

Chapter:

Character's Name and Personal Attribute	Quote from Text Showing This Personal Attribute
Name of character: Personal Attribute:	Page Number of Quote: Quote: " " Why this Quote Works:
Character's Name and Personal Attribute	**Quote from Text Showing This Personal Attribute**
Name of character: Personal Attribute:	Page Number of Quote: Quote: " " Why this Quote Works:

Sample Entry for Double-Entry Journal

Today's Date: *April 13*

Chapter: *15*

Character's Name and Personal Attribute	Quote from Text Showing This Personal Attribute
Name of character: *Opal* Personal Attribute: *considerate*	Page Number of Quote: *p. 100* Quote: *"I worried about him hogging the fan. "* Why this Quote Works: *This quote shows that Opal is worried that her dog, Winn-Dixie, is sitting in front of the fan and Miss Fanny might not get any of the cool air from the fan. Since it is Miss Fanny's library and her fan, Opal doesn't want her dog, who is a guest, to hog all the fan.*

Because of Winn-Dixie **Final Project**

As a culminating activity after reading Kate DiCamillo's *Because of Winn-Dixie*, you are to create a special poster for one character of your choice. The poster must contain a picture of the character exhibiting three physical traits that were mentioned in the story. These traits should be labeled and a quote from the text written by the label as "evidence." Underneath the picture, list five personal attributes of the character with a quote from the text to support each attribute. At the very bottom of the poster, write what is "bittersweet" for that character."

Checklist for Final Project

Name of Character:

Put a check mark by each step when you complete it.

1.   Picture of character.

2.   Three physical traits of character labeled on picture.

3.   Quote from text for each physical trait next to label.

4.   List of five personal attributes of character.

5.   Quote from text for each personal attribute labeled.

6.   Paragraph written on bottom of poster explaining what is "bittersweet" for the

      character.

Sources of the Reading Selection, Additional Readings, and Other Material

Sources of the Reading Selection

DiCamillo, Kate. *Because of Winn-Dixie*. New York: Candlewick Press, 2000. 182 pp.

DiCamillo, Kate. *The Tiger Rising*. New York: Candlewick Press, 2001. 116 pp.

Criticism/Book Reviews

Engberg, Gillian. *Because of Winn-Dixie*. Booklist. May 1, 2000, Volume 96, Number 17, p. 1665.

James, Helen Foster. *Because of Winn-Dixie*. School Library Journal. June 2000, Volume 46, Number 6, p. 143.

Because of Winn-Dixie. The Horn Book Magazine. July 2000, Volume 76, Number 4, p. 455.

Internet Sites

http://childrensbooks.about.com/parenting/childrensbooks/library/weekly/aa040801a.htm — Summary of chat with Kate DiCamillo.

http://www.authorchats.com/archives — Author chat on-line with Kate DiCamillo on May 29, 2001. Questions asked by students at John Muir Elementary in Washington.

www.bookjackets.com — A short bit of information about Kate DiCamillo on the favorite authors page.

Reference

Graves, M. F., Prenn, M. C., & Cooke, C. L. (1985). The coming attraction: Previewing short stories to increase comprehension. Journal of Reading, 28, 594-598.

Scaffolded Reading Experience™ for Fostering Higher-Order Reading and Comprehension Skills

with

"Black Powder"

by William F. Wu

An SRE™ Created by Cheri Cooke
University of Minnesota
© 2003 Seward Learning Systems, Inc.
Available at OnLine Reading Resources
onlinereadingresources.com

Table of Contents

Introduction

The best books break down borders. They surprise us—whether they are set close to home or abroad. They change our view of ourselves; they extend that phrase "like me" to include what we thought was foreign and strange.

—*Rochman,* Against Borders *(1993)*

Reading can inspire a generation of caring and tolerant citizens. Through good books, we can explore cultures and customs and foster mutual understandings.

—*Kaplan, United in Diversity: Using Multicultural Young Adult Literature in the Classroom (1998)*

These quotes suggest some of the reasons literacy teachers include multicultural books in their classrooms. Educators often choose multicultural literature as a means to help their students build connections with each other in increasingly diverse school environments. Teachers hope that multicultural literature may help create communities in which all peoples are valued and cultural differences are celebrated. Such are the reasons that "Black Powder" might become part of the language arts curriculum. The story, written by William F. Wu, is included in *American Dragons: Twenty-Five Asian American Voices*, an anthology edited by Laurence Yep.

William F. Wu is a Chinese American writer who lives in southern California. He has a Ph.D. in American Culture and has had a story adapted for *The Twilight Zone* TV show. He has written young-adult novels in Isaac Asimov's *Robots in Time* series. His book, *Hong on the Range*, was selected by the American Library Association as among the Best Books for Young People in 1989. One of his short stories, "Wong's Lost and Found Emporium," is included in *A Century of Fantasy 1980-1989: The greatest Stories of the Decade*, a collection of fantasy and science fiction stories edited by Robert Silverberg.

"Black Powder" is truly a unique story. The setting is Star Hector Space Station, April, A.D. 2017. When the story opens, readers discover that the protagonist's father has died as a result of a computer error in a shuttle accident on the way to the Moon. The protagonist, a seventeen-year-old high school junior who has lived on the space station his entire life, has earned a high grade on an English paper. He is saddened that he cannot show the paper to his father. He then learns from his maternal grandfather, who has recently moved to the Space Station, that in the old days in Chicago's Chinatown people sent things to those who had passed on to the afterlife through elaborate ceremonial procedures.

The protagonist, an Episcopalian, asks his grandfather to help him plan a memorial service, the details of which are planned to match a service based on Chinese folk religion. The service requires incense and fireworks, and the protagonist must ignore rules of the space station to locate or create the necessary items to honor his father and send the paper to the afterlife. He eventually makes contraband fireworks in a chemistry lab on the station. He then builds a shrine, burns money for the spirit world, and sends his assignment to his father.

As students read, they will learn about the traditions upon which these actions are based. They will also be reminded of the traditions and beliefs that bring meaning and value to their own lives.

Objectives

- To introduce students to the social, religious, and cultural aspect of China through reading activities

- To develop an appreciation for the character whose life is very different from the student's

- To learn the value of the past and to appreciate its influence on the present

Higher Order Thinking Skills

- Applying — Carrying out or using a procedure in a given situation.

- Evaluating — Making judgments based on criteria and standards.

- Creating — Putting elements together to form a coherent or functional whole, reorganizing elements into a new pattern or structure.

Chronological List of Activities

Day 1

Prereading Activities

(1) Motivating, *20 minutes*

(2) Relating the reading to the students' lives, *5 minutes*

(3) Building text-specific knowledge about "Black Powder", *5 minutes*

(4) Pre-teaching vocabulary that is relevant to "Black Powder", *10 minutes*

(5) Direction Setting, *5 minutes*

Day 2

During-Reading Activities

(1) Read aloud to students, 3 minutes

(2) Read aloud by students, 3 minutes

(3) Class discussion, 5 minutes

(4) Silent Reading, 24 minutes

(5) Guided reading exercises, *10 minutes*

Day 3

During-Reading Activities

(1) Class discussion, *15 minutes*

(2) Silent reading, *20 minutes*

(3) Guided reading exercises, *10 minutes*

Day 4

During-Reading Activities

(1) Silent reading, *7 minutes*

(2) Guided reading exercises, *3 minutes*

Post-Reading Activities

(1) Class discussion on student answers to *Reading Guide*, *15 minutes*

(2) Class introduction to topic and questions for *Discussion Guide*, *10 minutes*

(3) Small group discussions, *10 minutes*

(4) Class discussion on unanswered group questions, *15 minutes*

Day 5

Post-Reading Activities

(1) Test, 30 minutes

(2) Class discussion on exam, *15 minutes*

Detailed Description of Activities

Day 1

Prereading Activities

1. Motivating Activities, 20 minutes

- Begin the class by projecting computer images of the International Space Station on a large screen in the front of the room.

- Explain to the students: "Today, we are going on a fieldtrip to the International Space Station. Here is some background information before we join the Station."

- Display the following link; project the various Space Station images:

  http://spaceflight.nasa.gov/gallery/images/station/animstills/LWSindex3.html

  Note: if you cannot view or find this image, search for "Space Station: animation stills" from the main NASA website (www.NASA.gov).

- Display the following link; project the pictures and text within *The International Space Station: An Overview* (NASA, 1999) document:

  http://www.jsc.nasa.gov/er/seh/issovw.pdf

  Read the first paragraph of the document. Provide a brief description of the project to the students, the launching date of the first two components, and the countries involved in building the station. Then, display pictures from the 6 pages of the document.

- Explain to the students: "Now, let's see what the station will look like after it is assembled and as it orbits the earth. I will show you views from NASA's website."

- Click to the Internet sites listed below, display the pictures, and read the descriptions to the class:

  - This digital artist's concept shows a close-up of Russian segments of the International Space Station after all assembly is completed in 2003:
    http://spaceflight.nasa.gov/gallery/images/station/artistconcept/html/s97_10540.html

  - Commander Bill Shepherd of the first International Space Station crew is visible as he inspects the interior of the Russian Service Module recently at the Rocket Center factory in Moscow. The Service Module will provide living quarters and life support systems:

http://spaceflight.nasa.gov/gallery/images/station/crew-1/html/97_16433.html

- Computer Generated Still—Close-up of Transhab Module crew quarters.
  Transhab is to be installed on the International Space Station:
  http://spaceflight.nasa.gov/gallery/images/station/transhab/html/s99_05360.ht
  ml

- International Space Station sunrise view. Animation Still Image:
  http://spaceflight.nasa.gov/gallery/images/station/animationstills/html/s97_105
  39.html

- International Space Station overview. Animation Still Image. Daytime view:
  http://spaceflight.nasa.gov/gallery/images/station/animationstills/html/s97_105
  38.html

- International Space Station overview. Animation Still Image. Two nighttime
  views:
  http://spaceflight.nasa.gov/gallery/images/station/animationstills/html/s97_105
  36.html and
  http://spaceflight.nasa.gov/gallery/images/station/animationstills/html/s97_105
  37.html

- Ask the following of the students:

  - What do you suppose actually living in a space station would be like?
  - Do you know that scientists have been studying how to live in space for more
    than two decades?

- Explain to the students: "NASA says that many advances have been made. For
  example, air on the Space Shuttle is cleaner than on the Earth. Meals on the Space
  Shuttle are tasty and nutritious. But, there are still problems for travelers to space.
  For example, weightlessness and its effects on the body still are not completely
  understood."

2. *Relating the reading to the students' lives, 5 minutes*

- Explain to the students: "Now, imagine the future, year 2017. Scientists have solved
  many life-in-space issues. They have solved weightlessness problems and other
  health issues. Let's imagine that it is possible to have whole communities living in
  space, sort of like cities."

- Ask the students:

- What would you would need for a community and environment like this to be safe and comfortable?
- Would you need some laws?
- What kinds of laws might you need?

3. Building text-specific knowledge, 5 minutes

- Explain to the students:
    - Today you will read a story called "Black Powder." The story is set in the year 2017, on Star Hector Space Station. As you read, you will be transported to a future space station where people are able to live comfortably without ever returning to Earth. In fact, the main character, Tom Leong, a 17-year old high school student, has spent his entire life in this station in space.
    - You will learn about Tom's life and about his family. Tom's father, known as the 'elder' Tom Leong has recently died in an accident. Young Tom feels that the memory of his father requires a better funeral service than was provided by their Episcopal Church on Star Hector. The story tells about what young Tom does to plan and provide a new and better service for him.
    - You will meet young Tom's mother, Ellen, and his grandfather, Alvin. Tom discusses plans for the memorial service with them. You will also discover that parts of his plan are illegal in the space station community where he lives.
    - The details of the service may be very different from anything you have experienced in your life. You need to know that young Tom makes his plan based on what his grandfather tells him of ceremonies and rituals from China.
    - Be alert and focus as you read. You will learn about the future possibilities, and, also, experience the past from ancient China.

4. Pre-teaching Vocabulary Activity, 10 minutes

- Explain to the students: " Words which might be new to you are on the following overhead transparency."
- Display an overhead transparency with the following words, page numbers, and sentences from the story:
    - *wok:*
      "This is a zero-gravity wok" (p. 213) A wok is a large, thin metal pan with a round bottom.
    - *stir-fry:*
      "You stir-fry in it" (p. 213). In stir-frying, the food is cut into small pieces and

cooked in a small amount of fat. The cook fries the food at a high temperature for only a few minutes and stirs it constantly with a tossing motion. This definition applies to earth. You will have to read the story to find out how this is different in space!

- *Chinatown:*

  "Maybe somebody ought to start selling these down in Chinatown. Make a fortune" (p. 214). Chinese immigrants who have moved to America often have lived in city neighborhoods called Chinatowns. Chinatowns can be found in Chicago, Los Angeles, New York, and San Francisco. Alvin Kwok, young Tom's grandfather, grew up in Chicago's Chinatown.

- *concentric:*

  "The wheels are concentric" (p. 215). Concentric means having the same center. A number of wheels that are concentric would all have the same center.

- *centrifugal force:*

  "The faster they go, the more centrifugal force creates artificial gravity against the far inside wall, which is the floor here" (p. 215). This is a concept from physics which refers to the movement of objects. An object moving around a circle is actually being pulled toward the center.

- *Episcopalians:*

  " 'We're Episcopalians,' said Tom" (p. 220). Episcopalians belong to the Episcopal Church, a Christian denomination in the United States.

- *incense:*

  " 'We need firecrackers and incense' said Alvin" (p. 224). Incense is a mixture of substances that when burned, gives off a sweet smell. It has been—and is still used—at religious ceremonies. The ancient Egyptians, the Greeks, the Romans, and the early Christians burned it. The burning of incense is still part of the ritual of the Eastern Orthodox Churches, the Roman Catholic Church, and some of the Episcopalian churches. Buddhists also burn incense during religious ceremonies.

- *contraband:*

  "slipping his contraband into his pockets" (p. 229). Contraband refers to something smuggled or against the law to have.

- Read each word and sentence listed on the transparency. After each term, ask the following questions:

  - Does anyone know what this word means?

132

- o   If you don't know, can you figure out the meaning of each word by the way it is used in the sentence?
- o   If not, read the synonyms provided above.
- Hand out the Reading Guide for "Black Powder".

5.   *Direction Setting, 5 minutes*

- Explain to the students: "Now we will begin. As you read, you will discover the detailed plans young Tom makes for the memorial service. You will also discover how Tom becomes more understanding of his family's heritage. Please read carefully. You will have a quiz when we are done."

Day 2

During-Reading Activities

1.   *Reading and Class Discussion, 10 minutes*

- Begin by reading the story aloud to the students for two pages (pp. 211-212).
- Have student volunteers read aloud to the students for three pages (pp. 213-215, and top of 216). Have one student read as the voice of young Tom, another to read the voice and thoughts of Alvin Kwok, and another to read the voice and thoughts of Ellen.
- Ask the students: "Based on what we have read so far, what do we know about life on this space station?"

2.   *Silent Reading with Reading Guide, 35 minutes*

- Hand out the students' *Reading Guide.*
- Explain to the students: "The *Reading Guide* contains questions about details in the story. Thinking about each of them will help you understand the story. Please read the story and respond carefully."
- Students will complete the *Reading Guide* questions, as they read the story silently, and then share responses with the entire class.

Day 3

During-Reading Activities

1. *Class Discussion, 15 minutes*

- Review the students' *Reading Guide* responses.

- Discuss what the students have completed in the guides thus far.

- Explain the following to the students:

   □ When I first read the story, I wondered what traditions Alvin was following. We read on page 219 that he would have burned Tom's English paper so that his father could have it. Then, he explains this is a belief from the old religion—the Chinese folk religion, from Chinatown.

   □ Let me project pictures from some interesting Internet sites explaining what the Chinese folk religion is. Information from these sites will help you understand the story.

- Display the following site, and then click on the *Introduction* link: http://www.csupomona.edu/~plin/folkreligion/chinesefolkrel.html

- Read the following passage:

   Folk religions have been practiced alongside Buddhism, Confucianism and Taoism by Chinese people throughout the world for thousands of years. Worship, legends, festivals and various devotions associated with different folk gods and goddesses form an important part of Chinese culture even today. (Chinese Folk Religions, 1998)

- Explain to the students: "Look at the list of gods on the left side of the page. Let's read about the Kitchen God, the Three Gods, and Festivals."

- Link to each of the following three sites. Display the pictures of the various folk gods, read the first part of the descriptions, and discuss comments the students may have:

   □ A site on Chinese folk religion: http://www.fccj.com/LearningResources/chi-reli.htm

   □ A site that explains the belief in three religious relationships, man and nature, relationship between man and man (dead or alive), and the relationship between life and the afterlife: http://www.fccj.com/LearningResources/chi-defi.htm

- A site that explains the importance of ancestors in Chinese culture: http://www.fccj.org/LearningResources/chi-elem.htm.

- Read aloud the following passage found on the last site:

  Ancestor Worship
  This is the most important form of Chinese religion. It is widely practiced across the entire society. The rituals concerning ancestor worship are very complicated and have to be followed precisely. Although it has been simplified in modern time, it will never fade away from the Chinese community.

- Explain to the students: "Finally, I want to read to you from a book about China. Listen to these statements about Chinese beliefs."

- Read the following quote aloud:

  Folk Beliefs:
  Many Chinese believe in gods and lesser spirits, such as the spirits of mountains and lakes. The people aim to live in harmony with the spirits and avoid offending them, or else find ways to appease the angry ones. Ancestor worship is another ancient custom based on the belief that the dead go to another world. It is the duty of the living to take care of dead ancestors, so paper "money" is burned as an offering, and food is placed at graves.

2. *Silent Reading with Reading Guide, 30 minutes*

- Have students continue reading the story and completing the *Reading Guide* for the remainder of class.

Day 4

During-Reading Activities

1. *Silent Reading with Reading Guide, 10 minutes*

- Have students continue reading the story and completing the Reading Guide for the remainder of class.

Post-Reading Activities

1. *Class discussion and complete Reading Guide, 10 minutes*

- Ask volunteers to read their answers for the class when students finish reading and the *Reading Guide*.

- Hand out the *Discussion Guide*.

- Have students read aloud the quotes at the beginning of the *Discussion Guide*.

- Discuss any questions or comments students may have about the quotes.

- Have students write their answers to the four questions in the *Discussion Guide*.

- When students have finished writing the answers, conduct small group discussions.

2. Small Group discussion, 10 minutes

- Divide the class into eight small groups.

- Ask the students to chose a facilitator and a reporter within the group.

- Students will read aloud their responses to the *Discussion Guide*.

- Assign one of the *Discussion Guide* questions to each group.

- Ask the reporter, for each group, to summarize the group's discussion for the assigned question to the entire class. Thus, the entire class will hear the views of two groups for each question.

3. Class discussion, 15 minutes

2. Discuss the group answers from the previous activity.

Day 5

Post-Reading Activities

1. Exam on "Black Powder," 30 minutes

3. Have students complete an exam that you write on the story.

2. Class discussion on exam, 15 minutes

4. Discuss any students' questions or comments about "Black Powder."

Student Materials

Student Materials for this SRE are two guides:

- Reading Guide for "Black Powder." This is a list of questions and instructions which students follow as they read.

- Discussion Guide for "Black Powder." The discussion guide will provide quotations from non-fiction sources to help students understand some of the history and facts behind this science fiction story.

Reading Guide for "Black Powder"

*Name*_____

The purpose of this guide is to help you understand the story by keeping track of details and events as you read. Please answer the questions. They are written in the order they appear in the story and are included so that you stop to think as you read.

(1) List the names of the characters you meet in the story. Next to each name, write down one important detail about his or her life.

(2) **Page 219-220**: Summarize what Alvin explains to young Tom about the "Chinese folk religion." Based on what he has learned, what does young Tom decide to do?

(3) **Pages 223-229**: List the supplies young Tom needs to perform the memorial ceremony. Then, state how he found or made each one.

(4) **Page 229**: Briefly describe the arrangements Alvin and Ellen set up by the back wall of the living room.

(5) **Page 230-233**: List the actions or steps that took place during the memorial ceremony. As you list each action or step, state who performed it.

(6) **Page 233-234**: How did Alvin feel after the ceremony?

(7) **Page 234**: How does young Tom feel at the end of the story?

(8) List here any questions you have about the story:

Discussion Guide for "Black Powder"

Name_____

Below are quotations from non-fiction sources to help you understand some of the history and facts behind this science fiction story.

About "Black Powder"...

Rockets were invented by the Chinese around 1200 AD. These first rockets used black powder, or something similar to it, as the propellant. (U. S. Army, 2001)

The Chinese certainly were the first to use black powder and, therefore, probably the first to use rockets as well....The ingredients of black powder—technically, it should not be called gunpowder...but it usually is—are charcoal, sulphur, and saltpeter. These have been known in China for perhaps two thousand years. The first firecrackers may have appeared in the Chin Dynasty (221-207 B.C.) or during the Han Dynasty (206 B.C.-A.D. 220). (von Braun & Ordway, 1975, p. 23)

A Tribute to the Chinese...

Today we see examples of Chinese inventions around the world...suspension bridges, canal locks, dike and levy systems on our rivers, oil derricks, the spinning wheel, even umbrellas. From kites to Chinese medicine, from fireworks to wheelbarrows, from spinning wheels to sailing ships, Chinese inventions changed our world. (Williams, 1996, p. 47)

An Interview Between an American Teenager and a Chinese Scholar...
American: We learned in school that the Chinese have...been a people who follow reason, and they do not have the same prejudices and superstitions as people in the West. Our teacher told us the Chinese had no time to think about the way of the gods.
Chinese: That is another misunderstanding about the Chinese....Over the centuries Chinese...were deeply concerned about mystical forces and the supernatural. Spirits and gods were thought to be everywhere even if they were not seen. The largest and most ornate building in every town usually was a temple and along the roadway and even paths in the fields, there were small shrines holding effigies of various deities. Virtually every house had at least one altar and place of sacrifice. Spirit gates stood just inside the entrance of family compounds to prevent the entry of evil spirits. And in any town or village, regardless of the day of the year, a visitor could see incense and spirit-money burned, food sacrificed and firecrackers exploding. (Eastman, 1988)

About Communicating with Those Who Have Died...

The relationship of the living to the dead is maintained...through ritual. Some rites are designed to gain knowledge about the dead: their whereabouts, how they are getting along, and when they will be reincarnated. Some rites are intended to provide comfort for the dead: the offerings of food, clothing, and money.... It is clear...that the attitude of the living toward the dead and that of the dead toward the living are functionally one. The relation of the living with the dead is...modeled upon that of the living with the living. (Hsu, 1971, p. 245)

Ancestor worship is...an ancient custom based on the belief that the dead go to another world. It is the duty of the living to take care of dead ancestors, so paper "money" is burned as an offering, and food is placed at graves. (Noi, 1998, p. 27)

My father and mother have taught me that it is important to honor our ancestors. Ancestors are the relatives who have lived before us, such as our grandparents and great-grandparents. On special days, we light incense in front of a picture of my grandparents. (Quinn, 1996, p. 21)

About the Ceremonies...

Chinese history began with the founding of the Xia dynasty in 220 B.C. By then, the Chinese had begun ancestor worship, or the offer of sacrifices to the dead to make sure they had a happy afterlife. Only male descendants could make these sacrifices, so it was important for families to have a son. (Noi, 1998, p. 10)

About Respect...

In China, children are taught to respect people who are older than they are. There was a time when Chinese children were expected to obey their elders without questioning. This tradition has relaxed somewhat, but elderly people are still held in high regard. This respect doesn't end when a child grows up; elderly people are looked up to for their wisdom and experience by people of all ages. In fact, the grandfather is considered to be the head of the family. (Pitkanen, 1990, p. 20)

About Chinese-American Teenagers Today...

Early Chinese immigrants who settled in Chinatowns practiced a folk religion. They built altars to honor the gods they worshiped back in China....Younger Chinese Americans not living in these...communities treat these ancient Chinese customs as magical superstitions, novel and entertaining in modern America. Influenced by Western advances in science and technology, today's Chinese Americans may balk at practices such as burning incense or kneeling at a temple. (Moy, 1995, p. 51)

Traditional Chinese may not literally believe in ancestral worship, but some continue to observe the rituals, including family feasts during certain holidays like Zing Ming, the Chinese Memorial Day, which usually falls in March or April. This is a day to honor ancestors by burning paper money or offering food. (Moy, p. 51)

For many younger Chinese Americans growing up in a Christian society, these beliefs are as foreign as they are to many other Americans. But the Chinese teach tolerance for all religions, something valuable for all cultures. (Moy, p. 52)

(1) Choose one of the previous quotes. How does it help explain details in the story?

(2) How does your family honor memories of those who are no longer living?

(3) What should our attitude be towards a culture that is different from our own?

(4) What could we do to develop positive attitudes towards a culture different from our own?

Sources of the Reading Selection, Additional Readings, and Other Material

Source of the Reading Selection

Yep, L (1993) *American Dragons: Twenty-Five Asian American Voices.* New York: Harper Collins.

Criticism / Book Reviews

http://www.cynthialeitichsmith.com/AsianAmbiog.htm — This website contains a review of *American Dragons: Twenty-Five Asian-American Voices*, the anthology that "Jijan" was published within.

http://hallamericanclassics.com/american/1668.shtml — This website contains another review of *American Dragons: Twenty-Five Asian-American Voices*, the anthology that "Jijan" was published within.

Internet Sites

http://www.csupomona.edu/~plin/folkreligion/chinesefolkrel.html — This website is a resource for Chinese folk religions.

http://www.fas.org/spp/military/docops/army/ref_text/chap2_im.htm — This website is an online resource, maintained by the US Army, with facts about space history.

http://www.fccj.com/LearningResources/chi-defi.htm — This website explains the belief in three religious relationships, man and nature, relationship between man and man (dead or alive), and the relationship between life and the afterlife.

http://www.fccj.org/LearningResources/chi-elem.htm — This website explains the importance of ancestors in Chinese culture.

http://www.fccj.com/LearningResources/chi-reli.htm — This website is a resource on Chinese folk religions.

http://www.globaled.org/issues/149/c.html — This website is an online resource for "Family, Fields and Ancestors," *in Issues in Global Education: Spotlight on China,* Eastman, L. E. (1988).

http://spaceflight.nasa.gov/gallery/images/station/animationstills/html/s97_10536.html — This is an online resource, maintained by NASA, with images on the International Space Station.

http://spaceflight.nasa.gov/gallery/images/station/animationstills/html/s97_10537.html — This is an online resource, maintained by NASA, with images on the International Space Station.

http://spaceflight.nasa.gov/gallery/images/station/animationstills/html/s97_10538.html — This is an online resource, maintained by NASA, with images on the International Space Station.

http://spaceflight.nasa.gov/gallery/images/station/animationstills/html/s97_10539.html — This is an online resource, maintained by NASA, with images on the International Space Station.

http://spaceflight.nasa.gov/gallery/images/station/artistconcept/html/s97_10540.html — This is an online resource, maintained by NASA, for an artist's conception of how the International Space Center looks.

http://spaceflight.nasa.gov/gallery/images/station/animstills/LWSindex3.html — This website is an online resource, maintained by NASA, images about the International Space Station.

http://spaceflight.nasa.gov/gallery/images/station/crew-1/html/97_16433.html — This is an online resource, maintained by NASA, with images on the International Space Station.

http://spaceflight.nasa.gov/gallery/images/station/transhab/html/s99_05360.html — This is an online resource, maintained by NASA, with images on the International Space Station.

http://www.jsc.nasa.gov/er/seh/issovw.pdf — This website is an online resource for NASA's PDF document library. See National Aeronautics and Space Administration's *NASA Facts: International Space Station: Overview* (Document No. IS-1999-06-ISS022) from this site.

References

Brittin, H. C. (1999). "Cooking," [CD-ROM]. *World Book Multimedia Encyclopedia*. Chicago, IL: World Book.

Episcopal Church (1999). "Episcopal Church," [CD-ROM]. *World Book Multimedia Encyclopedia*. Chicago, IL: World Book.

Hsu, F. L. K. (1971). *Under the Ancestors' Shadow: Kinship, Personality, and Social Mobility in China*. Stanford, CA: Stanford University Press.

Kim, H. (1999). Asian Americans [CD-ROM]. *World Book Multimedia Encyclopedia*. Chicago, IL: World Book.

Moy, T. (1995). *Cultures of America: Chinese Americans*. New York: Marshall Cavendish.

Mullen, P. A. (1999). "Incense," [CD-ROM]. *World Book Multimedia Encyclopedia*. Chicago, IL: World Book.

Noi, G. S. (1998). *Countries of the World: China*. Milwaukee, WI: Gareth Stevens.

Pitkanen, M. (1990). *The Children of China*. Minneapolis, MN: Carolrhoda Books.

Quinn, D. P. (1996). *Religions of the world: I am Buddhist*. New York: Rosen.

von Braun, W., & Ordway, F. I. (1975). *History of Rocketry & Space Travel (3rd ed.)*. New York: Thomas Y. Crowell.

Williams, S. (1996). *Made in China: Ideas and Inventions from Ancient China*. Berkeley, CA: Pacific View Press."